REALMS
OF
POWER

You are Powerful!!

Robert B. H—

(Acts 1:8)

REALMS
OF
POWER

OPERATING IN UNTAPPED
DIMENSIONS OF HOLY SPIRIT POWER

ROBERT HOTCHKIN

DESTINY IMAGE® PUBLISHERS, INC.
P.O. Box 310, Shippensburg, PA 17257-0310
"Promoting Inspired Lives."

This book and all other Destiny Image and Destiny Image Fiction books are available at Christian bookstores and distributors worldwide.

For more information on foreign distributors, call 717-532-3040.

Reach us on the Internet: www.destinyimage.com.

ISBN 13 TP: 978-0-7684-5774-2

ISBN 13 eBook: 978-0-7684-5775-9

ISBN 13 HC: 978-0-7684-5777-3

ISBN 13 LP: 978-0-7684-5776-6

For Worldwide Distribution, Printed in the U.S.A.

1 2 3 4 5 6 7 8 / 26 25 24 23 22

Dedications

THIS book is dedicated to Smith Wigglesworth, Maria Wood-worth-Etter, John G. Lake, Amy Semple McPherson, William Branham, Paul the apostle, and the many other men and women of God who have stirred and inspired so many of us to earnestly desire and zealously cultivate the realms of power available in Jesus Christ.

And most of all, it is dedicated to the Holy Spirit who makes it possible for every believer to move in power each and every day.

Acknowledgments

THE best books are way more than thoughts on a page. They are containers of wisdom, insight, and empowerment. A good book does much more than teach. It imparts and equips through experience, revelation, and anointing. When a book is successful it helps awaken, empower, and activate readers so that they can stand on the author's shoulders and become even more effective for God's Kingdom here on earth.

I hope and pray that *Realms of Power* is that kind of book. If it is, the credit goes to many more than me. I share it with those whose shoulders I stood on while writing these pages. They deserve to be acknowledged and heartily thanked.

My wonderful wife, Yu-Ree. Thank you for your love, support, and patience while I spent so many hours working on *Realms of Power*. I love you, appreciate you, and am grateful for the friend and ally that you are. You are all together lovely.

Ron and Patricia King. Anything I ever do for the Kingdom will always also be unto your accounts in Heaven. From my early days as a new believer, you took me under your wings, poured into me, loved me, discipled me, and encouraged me. You fed me in the spirit, and in the natural, again and again. There are no better friends, mentors, or spiritual parents than you two.

Larry Sparks. You are way more than a publisher and a prophet, you are a true Kingdom man. The way you choose to put godly values and the people you work with above anything other than God, is an example to Christian businesspeople everywhere. Your gracious patience, understanding, and support when we hit pause in the middle of this project so I could fully come alongside my wife during her time of need, deeply touched both Yu-Ree and me. We are grateful to you, and grateful for you.

Kay Franklin, Lynn Reeb, and Melissa Crawford. You three amazing women of God were there for Yu-Ree and me as intercessors and friends throughout the journey of this book. You are mighty prayer warriors, and we mightily appreciate you.

Contents

Foreword

I HAVE always passionately desired the supernatural manifestation of God. Some of this hunger can be traced to my coming into the Kingdom of God during the "Charismatic Renewal" and the "Jesus Movement" days. These were times when the gifts of the Holy Spirit were being rediscovered and operated. The church had become very traditional and religious in its function with no real demonstration of power. It was the epitome of what Paul told Timothy in Second Timothy 3:5 (NKJV): *"having a form of godliness but denying its power. And from such people turn away!"*

When these movements occurred, we became aware of the power of the Holy Spirit again. This power was to manifest the love and kindness of who Jesus desired to be in our midst. As a 12-year-old boy, I was caught up in this wonder. It has been true for the duration of my life. This is why this book by Robert Hotchkin is of such importance. Learning to walk in *Realms of Power* should be necessary reading for any who desire these dimensions.

It is my persuasion that longing for, pursuing, and operating in the power of the Lord should be a nonnegotiable attribute of any believer. We can see from Scripture that experiences in the power of the Lord is to establish our faith. First Corinthians 2:4-5 (NKJV) shows that the apostle Paul understood the necessity of this power in the believer's life:

> *And my speech and my preaching were not with persuasive words of human wisdom, but in demonstration of the Spirit and of power, that your faith should not be in the wisdom of men but in the power of God.*

Paul purposed not to amaze them with his oratory skills. He instead desired their faith to be in the demonstration of the Spirit and His power. This is the heart of God to this day. The lack of power being seen is a reason for weakness of faith among God's people today. If the power of God can become accessible and known, then we again will see a people who are unstoppable in their convictions.

In my book *Father, Friend, and Judge,* I make the case that there are many dimensions of the Spirit available to us. This I believe is what Jesus was primarily stating in John 14:1-3 (NKJV):

> *Let not your heart be troubled; you believe in God, believe also in Me. In My Father's house are many mansions; if it were not so, I would have told you. I go to prepare a place for you. And if I go and prepare a place for you, I will come again and receive you to Myself; that where I am, there you may be also.*

Jesus was not speaking of the building of a literal mansion in Heaven for us. In fact, the better idea being espoused here is that there are many dwelling places where God exists. Jesus was letting the disciples know that once His blood was shed and the Holy Spirit came and they walked in union with Him, they would have access into these dimensions. The encounters with Jesus would not be because *He came to where we were, but because we stepped into where He is.* This is why the statement, *"that where I am, there you may be also"* is of importance.

This is a fundamental adjustment in the way we think about encountering God and spiritual realities. What is impossible outside these dimensions, becomes possible within them. This is why *Realms of Power* is such a timely book. We are taught about these places in the Spirit and how to operate in them and from them. I know this book will help unlock each of us into new demonstrations of the Holy Spirit. We will be empowered to engage these places in the Spirit and see the resulting powers of God manifest.

Robert Henderson
Bestselling Author of *Court of Heaven* **series**

– 1 –

You Are Powerful

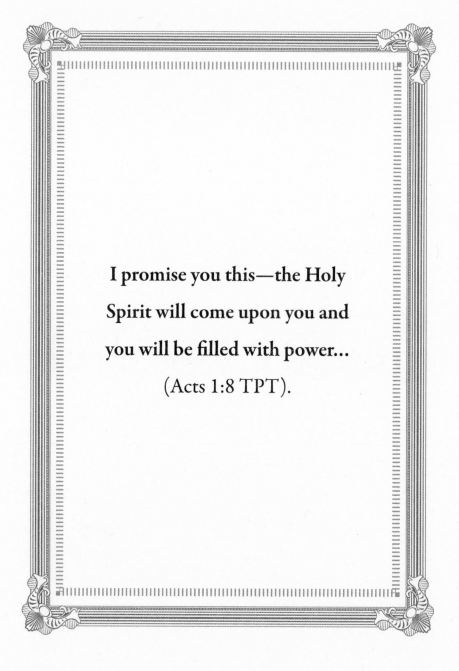

I promise you this—the Holy
Spirit will come upon you and
you will be filled with power...
(Acts 1:8 TPT).

THERE is a reason you are here right now.

I don't just mean there is a reason that you're sitting here reading this book. I mean there is a reason you're here on earth at this moment in history. God could've brought you forth anywhere, at any time. He chose here and now. The reason for that is simple—you are part of His solution on earth. He is very aware that you have a key role to play for the Kingdom right here, right now. He would very much like for you to be aware of this, as well.

The other thing He would like you to know is that you are well-equipped for the job.

See, God doesn't invite us to co-labor with Him in our strength, but in His. Just like with Joshua. When the Lord revealed the history-making role Joshua had to play in his day and age, God didn't just say, "Have a try at leading My people, son, and let Me know how it goes." No. He promised Joshua that no enemy would be able to stand against him because God would be with Joshua everywhere Joshua went (see Joshua 1:3-5). The Lord also promised that He would never fail or abandon him (see Joshua 1:5).

And that wasn't all.

God didn't just want Joshua to know that He, the Lord, was mighty. He wanted Joshua to know that because he walked with the Lord, Joshua was also mighty! In Joshua 1:9 (NLT 1996) the Lord spoke to Joshua, *"I command you—be strong and courageous!"* That command wasn't God issuing Joshua a high-pressure order to muster up some moxie so Joshua didn't disappoint the Lord by wimping out somewhere along the way. No. His command was actually an impartation of divine strength and courage. It was supernatural empowerment.

The Hebrew word used for *command* there in Joshua 1:9 is *tsavah* and it means "to appoint." It also means "to send with." God gave Joshua the supernatural power he would need to accomplish what he was being invited and sent to do.

I realize that was Joshua, one of the great heroes of the Old Testament. But it is the same for you today. No need to take my word for it. Take Jesus's. They're the words we started this chapter with from Acts 1:8. Read them again:

> I promise you this—the Holy Spirit will come upon you and you will be filled with power... (Acts 1:8 TPT).

The Lord makes it even more clear to New Testament believers in Acts 1 than He did to Joshua in the Old Testament. No need to do a word study on this one. It is right there plain as day. He promises that you *will* be filled with Holy Spirit power.

At the beginning of the book of Acts, the risen Lord is getting ready to release His disciples into all that He has won for them and made available to them through His complete, utter, and total victory over the enemy. He is getting ready to launch them out as the world changers and history makers of their day. Not in their power, mind you, but His. He promises to send His Holy Spirit to each and every one of them. Not just to brush up against them, or give them some tingles for a few moments here and there. But to fill them to overflowing with a never-ending abundance of everything they will ever need, wherever they go.

The victorious risen Lord is promising that those who are willing to believe Him and walk with Him will be empowered to put the reality of Him and His Kingdom on display on earth so that everyone has the opportunity to know that Jesus is real, that He loves them, and that He has overcome every oppression of the enemy for them.

One of the most exciting things about that promise in Acts 1:8 is that it wasn't just for those original disciples. It is an eternal promise for all believers for all time. It is for you right here, right now. The Lord promises that His Holy Spirit will come upon you and fill you with power. Divine power. Supernatural power. God power.

If you have said yes to Jesus Christ as your Lord and Savior, you are powerful. It's not an occasional thing—a flash here, a sparkle there. It's not just when you feel it. All of Heaven is available to you, all the time. You simply need to believe and step into it.

You are plugged into the Ultimate Power Source.

Every spiritual blessing in heavenly places is yours in Christ (see Ephesians 1:3). The apostle Paul wrote that truth to believers in Ephesus to make them aware that there was no need to wait until they got to Heaven to plug into heavenly power. They could do it right here right now. Paul wanted the church to realize that this was actually God's plan and desire.

Peter wrote similarly to believers in AD 66 to help open their eyes to the truth that everything pertaining to life and godliness was already theirs in Christ (see 2 Peter 1:3-4). All of God's rich and wonderful promises. For each of them. Right here right now. No lines to stand in. No waiting required. Peter even encouraged them to *"make every effort"* to see these gifts made manifest in their lives (see 2 Peter 1:5 NLT).

Again, it is the same for you. It is already all yours in Christ. All the realms of heavenly power and blessings. Right here on earth. Everything you need for this world, and to put the reality of Heaven on display in this world. Miracles. Healing. Favor. Provision. Protection. Joy. Peace. And much, much more.

You simply need to discover how to access all that power.

That's what this book is for. That's what you're here for. Get ready to plug in. Get ready to become a Kingdom-Come Conduit of Holy Spirit Power!

You can do this. I know you can. From firsthand experience.

THE GOD WHO LOVES AND EMPOWERS

I didn't really grow up with much talk about Jesus or the Bible. My parents took us to church on Christmas Eve and Easter. There were a few Sunday school classes. But that's all I recall. My mom and dad were both fine people, but I don't remember ever hearing either of them talk about the Lord, let alone His Word and promises.

By the time I was in my early teens I had gone through some stuff. I was angry, rebellious, and if someone mentioned God or the Bible to me, I made it clear I had zero interest. The nicest thing I did was to make fun of them. I spent most of my adolescent and adult life aggressively mocking and persecuting Christians and any form of the Christian faith and church. I used to tell anyone who would listen that "Christianity is a crutch for weak people who can't make it on their own."

Then, one day, Jesus showed up.

It was the fall of 2002. I was creeping up on my 39th birthday. And I was living on ten acres of Montana mountainside up in the woods of the

Flathead Range in the Northwest corner of the state. I had moved there to get away from it all after a fairly successful career on the creative side of big-budget brand advertising. I still worked part-time, freelancing for a variety of ad agency creative departments around the country as a sort of "idea engine." They would send me marketing briefs on various products or brands, and I would send them back scripts and outlines for TV, radio, and print ads. The rest of my time I spent fly-fishing, sea kayaking, cross-country skiing, snowshoeing, and enjoying Northwest Montana.

Winters lasted anywhere from four to six months in that area, and the cabin I lived in was heated by a wood stove. So I spent a lot of time cutting down trees, chain-sawing them into logs, and then splitting wood to make sure there was always more than enough fuel for however long the snow and cold lasted.

I liked winters in Montana. Things slowed down even more, and got even quieter. My get-away-from-it-all spot became even more remote come mid-to-late October when the temperatures would drop and the snow would usually start flying. And I really liked splitting wood. It was good exercise; but even more, it was a great way to work out some of my decades of anger, aggression, and frustrations. Some days I would split wood until I was too worn out to feel anything other than tired.

The day Jesus showed up was one of those days.

All these years later it is a little hard to describe what was going on in my life back then. The best way to give you the quick version is to say that despite having achieved much of what I had been told my whole life was supposed to make me feel happy and secure, I didn't feel that way at all. I felt like I was constantly on an up-and-down ride of uncertainty and frustration. Like no matter what I had or what I achieved, there was still no real security. There were moments of happiness, but they never seemed to last. And there was always a sense that what mattered most could go circling down the drain at any moment. On top of all that—or, more likely, because of all that—I was also in the middle of yet another relationship drama. So, axe in hand, I was taking it out on the woodpile.

I had been splitting wood for well over an hour. I was getting tired, but I didn't want to stop. Not because I needed to pile up yet another rick of logs for the woodstove. More because when there was a task in front of me, I could simply focus on that and not have to think about anything else. So I kept going. Until I was so tired I could barely swing the axe.

I remember my arms getting rubbery. And I remember that last swing. I brought the axe down sloppy. It skipped off the top of the log, and came out of my hands—almost taking part of my foot with it. I stood there. Worn out. In more ways than one.

I took a few steps back, and sort of plopped down into a snowdrift like it was some winter-wonderland armchair. I don't know how long I sat there trying to be numb, trying not to feel anything, even the cold.

What I do remember is how quiet it got. Not just remote-Montana-mountains-in-the-snow quiet. Something well beyond that. It was like a dome of supernatural silence had come down and utterly enveloped me. In the midst of this "holy hush" I couldn't hear my usual cavalcade of thoughts, or my worries, or my anger or frustrations. What I could hear, though, was the all-of-a-sudden presence of the Lord speaking directly to my heart.

"I refuse not to love you."

The God I had mocked and made fun of. The God I had denied. The God I had dismissed over and over again as a myth or a fable or a con. The God whose people I had persecuted. Jesus Christ. He sovereignly manifested His presence. He came to me. And all He wanted me to know was that no matter what, He was going to love me forever, and there was nothing I could ever do or say to make Him stop.

In that infinitely eternal moment of His presence, the Lord and I had a heart-to-heart conversation. I brought before Him every mean, selfish, wicked, arrogant, hurtful, hateful thing I had ever done in my 38-plus years. So many things. Any one of which, I felt, should have disqualified me in His eyes. Yet His answer to every single one of them was, *"I refuse not to love you."*

It undid me. I felt accepted. I felt loved. For the very first time in my life, I felt safe. Certain. Secure. Not based on me and what I could do or earn or achieve or convince or make happen. But based on Him, what He is like, and how undeniably trustworthy He is.

There's more to the story. But the point is that when the Lord showed up to declare the fullness of His love and goodness to me, He wanted to make sure that I knew it was not about what I was worthy of, or had earned. It was about Him. All about Him.

His love. His acceptance. How He looked at me. How He felt about me. My salvation. None of it was based on what I could achieve or make happen. None of it was because of something I had done, or ever could do. It was all about Him—who He is and what He is like.

GOD HAS GIVEN US EVERYTHING

This is how every believer comes into a saving knowledge of Jesus Christ. The stories of our salvations may differ, but the truth behind them is all the same. At some point each of us came to realize that Jesus is real, He loves us, and He gave His life for us—not based on who we were or what we were like, but totally based on who He is and what He is like. Each of us realized that we could not earn our salvation, and we rejoiced in the truth that we didn't have to because Jesus had done all, won all, and given all in the certainty of His love for us.

It is the same with His gifts, blessings, promises, and realms of power. He gives them all to us freely. From the get-go. We can't earn any of them, and we don't have to. Just like with our salvation, we simply have to believe and receive. It's all from Him. It's all through Him. It's all because of Him. Which is why we can always be certain that it is all ours.

The truth regarding the realms of power He has blessed us with became as real to me as the certainty of my salvation in a field outside of Nazret, a town in central Ethiopia.

I'd been a Christian for a few months. Some new friends invited me to go with them to a big conference in Seattle where I saw the miracle power of God put on display through several of the speakers. When these men prayed, sickness bowed, the lame walked, and all sorts of other profound things happened. With person after person. Right before my eyes. To be blunt, it was hard to get my head around it, but it was even harder to deny. I wasn't sure what to make of it all. God had a plan.

That plan ended up with me, about six weeks later, being part of a miracle crusade in Ethiopia. For ten days and ten nights I saw the Lord do amazing things. I saw tumors disappear. I saw blind eyes open. I saw the deaf hear. I saw a little girl, who was so demon-possessed that she threw me and one other man around like we were toys, get totally set free. I saw a man who was so sick he was brought to the crusade in an ambulance, and to the stage on a gurney, be totally healed and restored.

I saw God make a way for us to feed and care for the poor even when local officials confiscated an entire shipping container of food and supplies we had sent over before we arrived. I saw the Holy Spirit fall upon a crowd of thousands who then erupted into some of the most joyful dancing, praise, and worship of Jesus Christ that I have ever been part of. And it all happened when I and some other normal, everyday Christians prayed.

Any of you reading this who know me well, know that there is nothing special about me. In other words, the miraculous things I saw in Ethiopia when I prayed did not happen because as a new Christian I had figured out some super-big secret on how to pray extra-powerful prayers. Not at all. It had very little to do with me. Other than my willingness to be there, pray, and believe. And I can't really take any credit for that either since Scripture declares that even the faith I had to show up and expect prayer to work was a gift from God (see Romans 12:3; Ephesians 2:8; 1 Corinthians 12:9).

It was all by the power of the Holy Spirit. It was all exactly like Jesus promised in Acts 1:8. Not just for me. Not just for new believers. Not just for those willing to go to the other side of the world. Not just for someone willing to be part of a big miracle crusade. It is for every person who ever says yes to Jesus Christ, and receives the baptism of the Holy Spirit. He comes upon us in power. Faith power. Miracle-working power. Favor power. Soul-winning power. Provision power. Power to shift atmospheres. Power to bear mighty witness of the reality of our heavenly Father and His supernatural Kingdom here on earth. Notable and remarkable power. Realms of power.

If you are a Christian, you are powerful!

GOD'S PLAN SINCE DAY SIX

For the first five days and 25 verses of Genesis 1, we see God create the earth and everything in it. Then in verses 26-28, He creates us and puts us in place to operate as His dominion stewards over all creation.

*Then God said, "Let Us make man in Our image, according to Our likeness; **let them have dominion** over the fish of the sea, over the birds of the air, and over the cattle, **over all the earth** and over every creeping thing that creeps on the earth." So God created man in His own image; in the image of God He created him; male and female He created them. Then God blessed them, and God said to them, "Be fruitful and multiply; fill the earth and subdue it; **have dominion** ..."* (Genesis 1:26-28 NKJV).

It's right there at the very beginning of Scripture. On Day Six, God created humans with a plan and a purpose. His desire from the get-go has been to have a people who are willing to be in relationship with Him, who will walk with Him, talk with Him, and operate as His agents of impact for the Kingdom on earth. God has not changed His mind about that plan.

Have you ever wondered why you didn't go home to glory as soon as you said yes to Jesus Christ as your Lord and Savior? Which, let's get real, seems like it would be a great deal. Get saved. Go to Heaven. No more challenges in this fallen world. No more of those John 16:33 trials and tribulations. None of that "light and momentary afflictions" stuff, or the "sufferings of this present time" (see 2 Corinthians 4:17; Romans 8:18). Being immediately lifted up and out of all that sounds pretty good, right?

But Jesus came to do something beyond that. Yes, absolutely, He came so that we may all have eternal life (John 3:16). Certainly He came to pay the price for our sins at the Cross of Calvary (see 1 John 2:2). And clearly the Son of God came as the Son of Man to do for us what we were not able to do for ourselves (see Romans 8:3-4). But what I want you to see is that in doing all of those absolutely glorious things, He not only saved us, He also restored us to the plan He has had for us since Day Six.

In Christ you have been restored to relationship with your heavenly Father and all of His Kingdom right here on earth. You are once again His dominion steward. You once again operate from the overlap between Heaven and earth in His deputized authority, by the power of His Holy Spirit. You did not immediately go home to Heaven as soon as you got saved because you have some really awesome things to do here. Jesus outlines this in Matthew 16:15-19 (NASB):

> *He said to them, "But who do you yourselves say that I am?" Simon Peter answered, "**You are the Christ**, the Son of the living God." And Jesus said to him, "Blessed are you, Simon Barjona, because flesh and blood did not reveal this to you, but My Father who is in heaven...and upon this rock I will build My church; and the gates of Hades will not overpower it. **I will give you the keys of the kingdom of heaven**; and **whatever you bind** on earth shall have been bound in heaven, and **whatever you loose** on earth shall have been loosed in heaven."*

Notice that Jesus says when you realize who He is and what He has done—once you know Him as Messiah and accept Him as Savior—He gives you the keys. It is still, of course, His Kingdom. But you are now His Kingdom agent on earth. You do the binding. You do the loosing. All by His power, and all to His glory, but you have a key role to play.

You are here to release Heaven into the earth. You are here to advance the Kingdom of God. You are here to heal the sick, raise the dead, cast out demons, and more. You're here to show hope to the despondent, joy to the miserable, peace to the anxious, provision to the needy, and freedom to the captives. You are here so those who do not yet know the truth of Jesus Christ may come to see just how real and loving and kind and generous and merciful and awesome He is. You are here to be His mighty witness.

That's why you need power. And thanks to the gift of His Holy Spirit you are filled to overflowing with power in abundance. Just like the Lord promised in Acts 1:8. Just like we see the early church was ignited with in Acts 2:2. That is all a clear picture of what you also received when you said yes to Jesus Christ and the baptism of the Holy Spirit.

Right here. Right now. You are filled with realms of power. Every spiritual blessing. Everything pertaining to life and godliness. All you need to be empowered, and to powerfully put the Kingdom of God on display. All of it is yours in Christ.

Do not let the devil lie to you and tell you it's selfish to want to discover how to tap into those realms of divine power. That's not worshipping experience. That's not seeking God's "hand" more than His "face" or "heart." Walking in all that God has given you is not self-serving. It is serving the purposes of the Lord. It is fulfilling God's plan since Day Six. It is how we walk out the Great Commission (see Mark 16:15-19; Matthew 10:7-8). It is doing exactly what the victorious risen Lord invites us to in Acts 1:8—bearing mighty witness of the fullness of His goodness!

Sometimes the amazing truth of Acts 1:8 gets a bit twisted into the idea that when Jesus said He was giving us power to be mighty witnesses of Him, that it was only the power to evangelize. Soul-winning is absolutely important. And Holy Spirit absolutely empowers us to reach the lost. But that doesn't mean we only have power to evangelize. It means all the heavenly power God has plugged us into through His Holy Spirit evangelizes. All of the gifts. All of the blessings. All of the fruit. Each and every realm of power. They *all* put the reality of Jesus on display. In our lives. And through our lives. Faith does. Miracles do. Joy does. Favor does. Love does. Healing does. They all bear witness of Him. That, too, is part of God's plan. He knows we need all of it. He knows that the world needs to see Him in a variety of ways. Because at just the right time, just the right power will be just exactly what is needed to help someone realize in a very personal and meaningful way that Jesus is real. That He is there. That He cares. That He can be trusted. And that they can turn to Him.

FROM BELIEVER TO DISCIPLE TO WORLD CHANGER

You are being invited to a very special walk with the Lord. It is the same invitation He gave to Simon, Andrew, James, and John in verses 19 and 21 of Matthew 4. He is inviting you to come and follow Him. Which is much more than an invitation to simply walk after Him. It is an invitation to walk *with* Him. It is an invitation to be His disciple.

Sometimes we use the terms "believer" and "disciple" synonymously. We shouldn't. They have subtle but very important differences.

Jesus did not say to Simon, Andrew, James, and John, "Come believe in Me." He said, "Come follow Me." Jesus could see that the four men believed in Him. Even we can see it. After all, there is no way those good Jewish boys are going to leave their family businesses for just some guy wandering through the neighborhood. Even if He was a rabbi. Something in them responded to the Lamb of God when He walked up to them. Jesus saw that they recognized Him as the promised Messiah. Jesus saw that they believed. So He invited them to take a step beyond being believers and become disciples. He invited them to walk with Him. And talk with Him. And be mentored by Him.

Just like Father God had done with Adam in the Garden in the cool of the evenings, Jesus was inviting them to not only believe in who He is, but to come be discipled in how to "do Kingdom" here on earth. Jesus invited them to learn how to access the realms of heavenly power available through Him so they could become dominion stewards—world changers for the Lord!

And now it's your turn. He is inviting you to the same journey.

Everything in this book is based on Scripture. Every realm of power. In every chapter. It's all in the Word of God. And it's all available to you in Christ.

As you read through these pages, ask the Holy Spirit to lead and disciple you just like Jesus led those original disciples. Ask Him to help you to see what you have been given, and to help you start moving in it.

The world is waiting. The lost are waiting. Your family, friends, and community are waiting. Whether they are fully aware of it or not, they all long for a revelation of the reality of Jesus here on earth. You have the power to put that on display. In your life. And through your life. It's all yours in Christ.

Are you ready to tap into those realms of power? Are you ready for your world to change so that you can go out and be a world changer?

– 2 –

Power of Faith

Now faith is the substance...

(Hebrews 11:1 NKJV).

A S we begin to open the realms of power available to you in Christ, we have to start with the power of faith. Because faith is key. You could even say that faith is *the* key that unlocks everything of the Kingdom here on earth. The power of faith is how you access every realm of power.

Consider your salvation. You came into the Kingdom through faith in Jesus Christ. That right there shows you the power of faith. You were shifted from darkness to light, from death to life, from unbeliever to believer in a single moment by the power of faith. You didn't save yourself by believing, but the salvation that Jesus had already provided for you at the Cross of Calvary was made real in your life by the power of faith. You believed. You received. It was made manifest. That is the power of faith.

You access every realm of power that the Lord has opened to you in your salvation the same way you accessed salvation itself. Through the power of faith.

FAITH IS A SUBSTANCE

The key to how this works is in Hebrews 11:1 where the Word of God points out that faith is a "substance." Some translations say that faith is our "assurance." Others say faith is our "certainty" or "confidence." But to my mind "substance" is by far the best translation because it gives the clearest understanding of how the power of faith works.

The Greek word describing what faith is in the original text of Hebrews 11:1 is *hupostasis*. It is made up of two root words. One that means "place" and "time." And another that can be translated with a variety of meanings including "abide," "covenant," "bring," and "establish."

What a vivid word picture that paints of how the power of faith works. When we choose to *abide* in the *covenant* of God we *bring* and *establish* all of His eternal promises into this *place* at this *time*. Why? Because faith is a substance.

If you catch this, you've really caught it all—because faith is not just belief. Faith is not just some stirred-up confident hope. Faith is even more than you being certain and assured. Faith is actually a substance. Like right now, as I type these words on my computer keyboard, I am wearing one of our Men on the Frontlines "I Make a Difference" t-shirts. It is not the idea of a shirt. It is not the hope of a shirt. It is not the promise of a shirt. It is not the passionate longing for a shirt. It is an actual shirt. Why? Because of the substance of cotton. Cotton makes the shirt real. I can see the shirt. I can feel the shirt. And if you were here with me, you could too. All because cotton is a real and tangible substance. Cotton brought forth this shirt so I could have it in my life. Thread by thread, the substance of cotton manifested this shirt in the here and now.

Very similarly, your faith is a substance. And it is powerful. Way more powerful than the substance of cotton. Or leather. Or rubber. Or steel. Or any other earthly substance. Because the substance of your faith can do something no other substance on earth can do. It can manifest the promises of God here on earth. That is actually its purpose. That is why God gave it to you.

FAITH BRINGS FORTH WHAT YOU KNOW IS ALREADY YOURS

Let me give you another picture of this.

When I was a kid I had a big tub of Legos under my bed. Now back then in the 1970s, Legos were different from how they are today. These days when I buy Legos for my nieces or nephew they come in a box with a picture on the package telling you what you can build with them. When I was young, you just got a whole bunch of Legos. Big ones. Little ones. Flat ones. Square ones. Rectangular ones. Thin ones. Thick ones. In all sorts of colors.

Whenever I chose to pull that tub of Legos out from under my bed, I could build anything I wanted with them. One day I might make spaceships. The next day cars. The next, castles or ray guns. Whatever I could "see" in my imagination, I could build. And the Legos made them tangible. Because of the Legos, what I made was more than an idea or a hope or even a belief. Block by block the Legos I used made those things "manifest." I could touch them. Hold them. They became real.

The substance of faith works the same way. You have been blessed with every spiritual blessing in heavenly places here on earth (see Ephesians 1:3). You have been given everything pertaining to life and godliness (see 2 Peter 1:3). It's not that you will be given those things one day in the sweet by and by. They are already yours in Christ. You can be certain of that (see 2 Corinthians 1:20). God is not withholding anything from you. He has done all. He has won all. He has given all. If you see it in His Word, it is yours!

Provision? Yours!

Favor? Yours!

Protection? Yours!

Healing? Yours!

Returned prodigal? Yours!

Victory? Yours!

Peace, joy, patience, compassion, love? Yours! Yours! Yours! Yours! Yours!

Each and every blessing, promise, fruit, gift and power of the Holy Spirit who is living inside you? All yours!

You use the substance of your faith to see them made manifest in your life. Just like those Legos. You pull the "tub of faith" out from "under your bed" and then Scripture by Scripture, truth by truth, decree by decree, the substance of your faith establishes them all in your life.

Believing = Receiving

Jesus Himself said that all you have to do to receive from Heaven into the earth is to know and believe that it's all already yours. In other words, He said all you need to do is use the power of faith you have been given in Him.

> *Therefore I say to you, whatever things you ask when you pray,* **believe that you receive them, and you will have them** (Mark 11:24 NKJV).

When Jesus pointed out that the key to receiving is believing, He wasn't saying that if we're good little Christians and have faith, our heavenly Father will reward our religious performance by bestowing something upon us that He was hiding behind His back until we pleased Him with our faith. No. Jesus was discipling us in how to move in the power of faith. He was revealing that when we know something is already ours, nothing can keep it from us. In that knowing, we choose to believe. Believing then activates the substance of our faith. That then brings, builds, and establishes the reality of what is already ours in the eternal realm into our earthly midst.

The key to believing is knowing. Knowing God said it. Knowing He does not lie. Knowing He has given all to us in Christ. And because of all that, knowing it is all already ours. Even if we haven't seen it yet. Or perhaps I should say *especially* if we haven't seen it yet. Because that is when we really need to tap into the power of faith.

The devil is a liar. You know that. But what you have to start to see is how he uses temporary facts to lie to us about eternal truth.

When our checking account is looking less-than for another month.

When our prodigal seems to be getting farther and farther away from God.

When another day of symptoms, or the latest medical report, seems to indicate that we are not getting any better.

Those are all times when the devil loves to jump in with his lies that those temporary circumstances are our eternal portion. The reason he does this is so you choose to stop believing. If he can lie you into not using the power of faith, he can keep you from receiving here on earth what is already yours in Christ.

Whenever we don't yet see the manifestation of a promise or gift or blessing, we have to make sure that we don't start to doubt that God has given it to us. That's fear. That's the opposite of faith. It is disempowering and counterproductive.

The key is to know that God has given us everything in Christ. That it is already ours. It doesn't matter what we see or don't see in the natural.

It matters what we see and choose to believe in the Word of God. If God said it, you can count on it. God has given you every spiritual blessing and everything pertaining to life and godliness, they are all yours. You have them. Believe it. Especially wherever and whenever it looks and feels like you do not yet have the promise. You do. God has given it to you. His Word says so. And He does not lie.

So it's not that you don't have it, it's just not yet fully manifest in your life. You simply aren't seeing it in the natural...yet. Choosing to believe the eternal truth over the report of your temporary circumstances is actually what generates the substance of faith that establishes what is already yours in the eternal realm here in the earthly realm.

Here is how the apostle Paul put it in his second letter to the Corinthians:

> For our momentary, light distress [this passing trouble] is producing for us an eternal weight of glory [a fullness] beyond all measure... (2 Corinthians 4:17 AMP).

Notice how Paul mentions a "weight" of glory. That's because when we choose to believe eternal truth over temporary circumstances, the substance of our faith kicks in to begin to produce here on earth what is already ours in the eternal realm. I know this can be challenging. Especially when those "light" and "momentary" distresses feel anything but light, and go on for what seems like way more than a moment. But when you choose to believe the truth that the promise *is* yours despite how things look and feel, that faith produces a weighty, glorious substance that actually works to manifest the eternal promise into this temporal realm.

It's a lot like money you have in the bank right now. You know it's there. Your monthly statement tells you it's there. But you don't actually see it in your hands...yet. To see, have, and hold that money, you need to withdraw it from the bank. If you knew and trusted that the money was in your account, you would not hesitate to drive to the ATM and enter your PIN code. And you would absolutely expect that money to come out of the machine so you could spend it.

Bank on it!

It's the same with every spiritual blessing, promise, and Word of God. You have them. The Bible tells you that you do. They are already yours in Christ. And when you choose to believe that, the power of your faith works like a divine PIN code that allows you to withdraw what you know is yours in the eternal realm. And you can continue to make "withdrawals" from your heavenly account until you have every last bit of that certain promise in your hands!

ACTIVATE THE POWER OF FAITH

Now that you are seeing and understanding the realm of power you have available to you through the substance of your faith, let's look at practical ways for you to activate the power of faith in your life.

1. Get in the Word.

Romans 10:17 (NKJV) says that *"faith comes by hearing, and hearing by the word of God."* The more time you spend in the Word, the more you will hear and see and know all that God has given you in Christ. Knowing that it's yours is most of the battle. Choosing to agree, declare, and decree that truth is how you use the substance of your faith to download it from Heaven into the earth. It all starts in the Word. When you see the promise there, you know it's yours, and you can expect to see it in your life.

2. Lift up your "eyes."

In Genesis 13:14 (NKJV) the Lord tells Abram to lift up his eyes *"from the place where you are"* so that he could see the promises of what God most certainly will bring him into. Sometimes we have to do the same to stir up the substance of our faith. When you are in the midst of one of those temporary challenges, the devil will try to get you to believe that it's always going to be like that. He's lying. Ask the Lord to help you lift up your eyes above your circumstances to see His eternal truth more than those current facts.

3. Speak it out.

When you need to stir up your faith, start to decree into your circumstances the truth of God's Word. Job 22:28 (King James Version) promises that if we *"decree a thing, it shall be established."* Not may. Not might. Not could. But it *shall* be. If you are not feeling well, decree the truth that you are healed by the stripes of Jesus (see Isaiah 53:5). If you're believing for your prodigal to be saved, start speaking the truth that you have called upon the name of the Lord, you are saved, and so is all of your household including that prodigal (see Acts 16:31). Speaking out the truth of God's Word actually works to stir up the substance of your faith and establish His promises in your life.

4. Rejoice and give thanks.

The New Living Translation of Philippians 4:6 tells us to thank God for all He *"has done."* This is powerful. Why? Because He has won all, done all, and given all. When we rejoice and give thanks for what God has already done—especially when we do not yet see it in our lives, family, or nation—we plug into the power of faith. We can celebrate that the Lord has healed us, given us the breakthrough, and met every one of our needs. Because He has. Giving thanks for what we know He has done, even when we do not yet see it, supercharges the production of the substance of faith in our lives.

5. Receive.

The power of faith is not only to believe. We are also to receive. So take some time to intentionally receive what you are believing for. See it in the Word. Ask the Lord to help you see it in the Spirit. Then see it being established in your life by the substance of your faith. Thread by thread. Block by block. Every time you choose to believe—and see and decree and rejoice—you are establishing that truth on earth and in your life. Receive it!

– 3 –

Power to Work Miracles

Now God worked unusual
miracles by the hands of...
(Acts 19:11 NKJV).

I REMEMBER the first time I ever saw a miracle. It was the spring of 2003.

I had only been a Christian for a few months. Everything was new to me. I was hungry for anything to do with God. So when two friends who were older and more experienced Christians invited me to ride the eight hours with them to a big conference in Seattle, I immediately said yes.

The first morning of the event, we were lined up outside the venue with hundreds of other people. I could feel a real excitement. I didn't know much about who the speakers or worship leaders were, but everyone else seemed to. And there was a buzz of expectation about what God was going to do through them over the weekend.

There was a very dear older lady near me in the line. She needed the help of a walker to move and to stand. She visited with me for quite some time while we were waiting. When she found out I was new to all of this, she gave me a small, wooden cross that she had made by hand. She also encouraged me to expect "something big" from God that weekend.

The event was powerful. But what I remember even more than the worship and preaching was the ministry. My friends had encouraged me to politely make my way up to the front when God started moving. I asked them why, and they told me that several of the ministers were quite experienced at working miracles and they wanted me to see how real and how powerful God was. They wanted me to see a miracle up close.

Boy did I.

I was only about ten feet away when I saw one of the speakers pray for a man who had a metal rod in his arm. What struck me was that when the speaker was done praying, there was a bunch of gray metallic powder in his hand that had not been there before. Well, that and the look of absolute wonder on the guy's face he had prayed for and who was now saying over and over again that he couldn't feel the metal rod in his arm. He was pressing all up and down his forearm, trying to find the rod. And he couldn't. He said the rod was gone. And so was the deep, aching pain that had been there just a moment before.

This minister prayed for person after person who had metal in their body. And they were all set free from pain. And many of them miraculously had the metal supernaturally removed from their bodies, and new bone or tissue creatively regenerated. One lady even testified that her surgery scar had disappeared.

And then the kicker came. Just to seal the deal.

I was walking around the venue, thinking about all I had just seen. Trying to make sense of it in my head. *Did that really happen? Was this all some kind of elaborate scam with more than a thousand people in on the con? If this was really real, why wasn't every media outlet in the city here covering what God was doing? Who wouldn't want to see this?*

Then, all of a sudden, I noticed the dear older lady from the line outside the venue that morning was walking toward me. Walking spryly. With a huge, beaming grin on her face. Without her walker. She told me that during the ministry time she had received prayer, and that the Lord had completely healed her hips. She couldn't stop walking around the auditorium. Or smiling.

As that dear lady shared her story with me, I could feel the presence of the Lord. Tears welled up in my eyes. I wasn't sure what to make of it all. I didn't understand. But I also sensed that I didn't need to. Truly He is the God of Wonders. He is real. He is powerful. And He works miracles. Through His people.

WE ARE SUPPOSED TO WORK MIRACLES

We all love reading about when Jesus opened blind eyes and deaf ears in the Gospels. Or when He healed the sick and cast out demons. We have no trouble believing He worked miracles. But sometimes we wrestle with the idea that *we* are to work miracles. Or even if we can.

We can. And we're supposed to. That's His Word!

As Christians, we have no trouble believing John 3:16. We know that we know that God so loved us, He sent the gift of His only Son so that none would perish and all might have eternal life. So why do we wrestle with John 14:12? Jesus Himself tells us that if we are believers we will do the works that He did, and even greater. We can believe God to deal with all the sins of all the world, but we have trouble believing that He wants to work a miracle through us? What's the deal with that?

The Bible is not a salad bar. We don't get to pick and choose what bits we like and what bits aren't going to go onto our plates. If we believe one part, we need to believe it all. If we believe we are saved by the Son, then we need to believe that in Him we can do exactly what He says we can. Work miracles. To the glory of His name.

Jesus not only told us that we can do the works that He did when He was here on earth, He went out of His way to get specific about what many of those works were. In Matthew 10:7-8 He flat-out says that we are to go out there and heal the sick, cleanse the lepers, raise the dead, and cast out demons. He tells us that wherever we go, we are supposed to declare that *"the Kingdom of heaven is at hand."* You know whose hand He is talking about? Yours!

We tend to call the fifth book of the New Testament the book of "Acts," but the full name is actually the "Acts of the Apostles." Everything done in that book is done by a believer. God wanted to make it clear to everyone who reads the Bible that if they walk with Him, they are meant to be a miracle worker.

The book of "Acts" is filled with example after example of believers just like you working miracles to bear witness of the reality and victory of Jesus Christ.

God included an entire book in the Bible to show that you can work miracles.

In Acts 3:2-7, Peter prayed for a lame beggar and immediately the man's feet and ankles were healed, strengthened, and restored.

In Acts 8:4-8 (NKJV), Philip was in Samaria. He *"preached Christ"* to the people of the city. And *"the multitudes with one accord heeded the things spoken by Philip."* You know why? Because of the miracles Philip worked in the name of the Christ he was preaching. Demon-possessed people were set free. The paralyzed and lame were healed. And there *"was great joy in that city"* despite the dark social and political times. All because Philip put on display how great and how real and how mighty Jesus truly is.

And then there is the Scripture we started this chapter with. Acts 19:11. Where we see that God was performing *extraordinary* miracles by the hands of Paul. How cool is that?!

Now before you start thinking, *Sure, but that was Peter and Philip and Paul. They were mighty men of God, pillars of the first-century church. I'm just me.* I want to point out to you that it says that God was performing the miracles through the hands of Paul. God empowered Paul to do it. And Peter. And Philip. And many other men and women in the Bible, and throughout church history. All God needs is a believer willing to step out. A believer willing to pray in faith that Jesus is who He says He is, has done what He says He has done, and has empowered us to put His reality on display to a world that desperately needs to see Him as much as hear about Him. All God needs is a believer willing to extend his or her hand, declaring the Kingdom of Heaven is here. A believer like you!

That's what the book of Acts is for—to help you see what God wants to do through a believer. He wants you to see what He can do through you.

Have you ever read a book on revival or one of the great revivalists, and thought, *I want to see that!* That is exactly how God wants you to respond. He wants you hungry to see the miraculous in and through your life. That's one of the reasons He raises up great men and women of God. He is putting on display how great He is through those men and women. In the hopes that even just one more will understand what He can do through him or her too.

Years ago when I was new in ministry I read every book I could find on historic revivals and the great revivalists. I found champions like John G. Lake, Smith Wigglesworth, and William Branham especially inspiring. I remember when I was reading the six-volume biography of Branham, I was about halfway through the second book when I was hit by all God had done through this man, even in the early years of his ministry. I wanted to see that level of the miraculous as an everyday occurrence in the church again.

I laid the book down and cried out to the Lord, "Where is the God of William Branham today?!" Almost immediately I heard the Lord answer deep in my heart, *"Where are My servants like William Branham today?"* I knew in that moment exactly what God was getting at. As He brought back to mind all I had read about Branham's humble early life in the first volume of the biography, I realized that God does not need the brilliant. He does not need the gifted. He does not need the influential. He does not need the best of the best, the wisest, or the most charming. He simply needs the willing. Those who are willing to believe His Word, willing to trust in His truth, willing to step out in the measure of faith they have been given, and willing to declare that the Kingdom of Heaven is at hand!

Are you willing? Then let's get you started.

ACTIVATE THE POWER TO WORK MIRACLES

Like with everything about the Kingdom here on earth, it all begins with knowing you already have all that you need in Christ.

For me it was Matthew 10:1. I remember sitting in my chair by the woodstove in my cabin up in the woods of Montana reading that passage of Scripture for the first time and getting so excited when I saw that Jesus gave His disciples authority to heal every disease and sickness. I actually jumped up out of that chair and declared to the roof timbers, "I am a disciple of Jesus Christ! That means He has given me authority to heal every sickness!" I couldn't wait to find someone to pray for.

In First Corinthians 12, the apostle Paul was mentoring the church to help give them their jump-out-of-the-chair revelation that they could move in power and flow in the gifts of the Spirit just like him. In verse 10 he let every believer know that the working of miracles is not just for well-known, traveling apostles. It is for everyone who has the Holy

Spirit of God. Paul comes right out and says that we have been given Holy Spirit power for the *"working of miracles."*

Note that Paul didn't say that we have been given power *for* miracles. He said it was power for the *working of* miracles. That very important detail is the key to unlocking this realm of power.

That word *working* is sometimes translated as "effecting," "perform," or even "acts." In the original Greek the word is *energeo,* and it has two very important meanings. The first is "to be mighty." The second is "to be active." Put the two meanings together and you get the key to unlocking this realm. If you want to be *mighty* in the working of miracles, then you simply need to be *active* in the working of miracles. The more you step out in faith, the more you will see. And even when you don't see something right away, being active in this realm is what helps you grow mighty in this realm.

Every minister I personally know who operates in any significant level and regular occurrence of the miraculous, went through a time when nothing seemed to happen, but they continued to step out and pray for people over and over again anyway. They did it because they knew who their God was, and what He had given them and called them to. So they prayed. Again and again. They celebrated even the tiniest of improvements. And one day, from being so active in the working of miracles, they saw an explosion of being mighty in miracles.

Before we move on, let me settle something that often comes up when I teach on this. It is not that being active in the working of miracles earns you a greater level of power or authority. It is that choosing to operate more regularly in the power and authority that you have, works to establish the realm more fully in your life.

Think of it like having a big, blue crayon. You will never see a page colored blue if you don't take it out of your box of crayons and use it.

You didn't earn the big, blue crayon by coloring with it more and more. You already had it. Coloring with that big crayon more often, simply worked to cover the page more completely. You grew more mighty in the manifestation of the color blue, by being more active in coloring with that big, blue crayon.

I can't promise that the first time you ever step out and pray for someone you will definitely see a miracle. But I can promise that if you never pray for anyone, you will never see God work a miracle through you.

The following are some practical ways for you to activate the power of working miracles.

1. Be on the lookout.

Find someone every day to pray for. You can be on the lookout for people with canes, casts, walkers, or wheelchairs who might need a healing miracle. Or simply start a conversation with someone by saying, "Hi," and then listen to what is going on in their lives. Maybe they need a financial miracle or a miraculous breakthrough in a relationship or work situation. Almost everyone has some situation in their life where they would love to see God show up. I would actually ask people that question during my miracle outreaches. I would listen to their story, let them know I genuinely cared, and then I would ask, "If God is as real as I know He is, where in your life would you most want Him to show up for you right now?" Over the years, many people who started out claiming they did not believe in God have let me pray with them from that simple approach.

2. Be expectant.

When you pray, believe and receive. Expect the miracle. And remember that every time you pray, something happens. I can't tell you the number of times I did not see an immediate miracle, but days, weeks or even months later I would get an email or a text with the good report of what our amazing God had done!

3. Never give up.

Keep being active in the working of miracles. If you do, you will grow mighty in the working of miracles!

– 4 –

Power of Unity

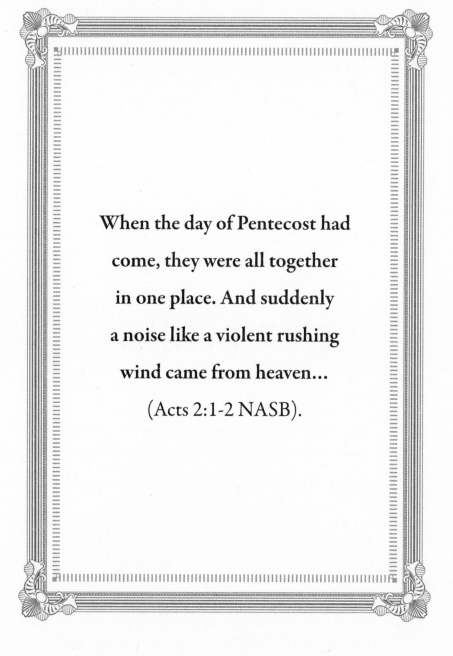

When the day of Pentecost had

come, they were all together

in one place. And suddenly

a noise like a violent rushing

wind came from heaven…

(Acts 2:1-2 NASB).

A FEW years ago I had an encounter with the Lord where He took me into Genesis 1. There were many aspects and layers to what He revealed to me during that time. One of the most profound was what He showed me about how creation was brought forth. We all see in those first 25 verses that God created the earth and everything in it. But what I had never really noticed before was *how* He created all of space and time in those first five and a half days. The Lord showed me that it was through a harmonious cooperation of divine unity.

The Holy Spirit hovered.

The Father spoke.

And the Word—whom we know from John 1:14 is the Son—went forth.

Our Three-in-One God—Father, Son, and Holy Spirit—brought forth all of creation through the power of unity.

I realize that the "Godhead" is a huge theological can of worms. And to be blunt, I really have no interest in opening that can beyond simply pointing out what the Bible clearly shows us in Genesis 1:1-25. In a divine, cooperative, harmonious agreement of His Three-in-Oneness, God brought forth all of creation. Then, in that same Three-in-One unity, He made us in His image and put us in place as His dominion stewards over all of that creation.

Look at Genesis 1:26-28 (NASB):

> *Then God said,* **"Let Us make mankind in Our image, according to Our likeness;** *and let them rule over the fish of the sea and over the birds of the sky and over the livestock and over all the earth, and over every crawling thing that crawls on the earth."* **So God created man in His own image, in the image of God He created him; male and female He created**

them. God blessed them; and God said to them, "Be fruitful and multiply, and fill the earth, and subdue it; and rule...."

We clearly see here that the Father-Son-Spirit "Us" of God made humankind—both male and female—in His Three-in-One image to rule and reign on earth as His deputized agents of authority. The reason this is so key is that one of the things the Lord helped me understand during my Genesis 1 encounter with Him was that the first 25 verses of the Bible are not only a history lesson of how He brought forth creation, but also a model of how we are to steward His creation over which He has put us in charge.

The "Us" of God brought forth creation through the divine power of unity. And because we are made in His image, we are most effective in stewarding creation when we also operate in the divine power of unity. First and foremost, each of us is united with God by being in relationship with our Father through the gift of His Son as we walk in the power of the Holy Spirit. But then, also, each of us believers is choosing to walk in unity with one another as the Body of Christ on earth.

MORE POWERFUL TOGETHER

Any man or woman with God is "in the majority." All we have to do is look at Elijah on Mount Carmel to see the reality of that. First Kings 18 shows us that when a believer walks with God, it doesn't matter how many are against him or her. When you're with God, the numbers are on your side. Even if it is "just" the two of you.

And yet God also makes it clear that something profound happens when we not only choose to cooperate with Him, but also choose to be in unity with one another. A geometric multiplier of exponential increase supernaturally happens through the power of unity. It is right there in Deuteronomy 32:30 when it points out that one can chase away a thousand enemies, but when two come together they can make 10,000 flee.

The Kingdom impact of two believers in unity does more than double. It increases by a power of ten. Now imagine what happens with three, four, a dozen, or hundreds? Imagine when the global church wakes up to the power of unity and chooses to stop attacking one another, and instead all that energy goes toward working together to attack the enemy.

We see something similar in Psalm 133:2-3 where it talks about how good it is for believers to be in unity. Unity causes the power of the anointing to flow (see verse 2). Unity brings refreshment and renewal (see verse 3). And most of all, when we choose to co-labor and cooperate in unity, the Lord actually commands a blessing in our midst (see verse 3). It's not just that He *releases* a blessing, He *commands* one. Like when He commanded in Genesis 1:3, *"Let there be light."* It comes forth and nothing can stand in its way. Powerful!

In his New Testament Epistles, the apostle Paul reminds the church of the power of unity again and again. He warns not to allow division in our midst (see 1 Corinthians 1:10). He speaks repeatedly of honoring differences of focus and assignments, while still co-laboring together as one body for Christ (see Romans 12:4-5; 1 Corinthians 12:12-13; Ephesians 4:16). He even says to flat-out avoid anyone who tries to create dissension or discord among believers (see Romans 16:17).

Acts 2 may be the best New Testament example we have of the power of unity. When 120 people with different histories and from different backgrounds chose to gather together in unity, it made place for a massive flow of heavenly power to explode into the earth (see Acts 2:1-2).

On the Day of Pentecost, God clearly put on display how He commands a blessing in the midst of believers who choose to co-labor and cooperate on behalf of the Kingdom.

UNITY DOESN'T JUST HAPPEN, IT'S A CHOICE

We've read the Bible. We all know that the Acts 2:2 move of God broke out after ten days of united worship, prayer, and praise. But the 120 who gathered in the Upper Room there in Jerusalem didn't know it would take a week and a half to happen. All they knew is that the risen Lord had invited them to "tarry" for a "few days" to receive the promise of the Father (see Acts 1:4-5). Ten is way more than a "few." I guarantee that interpersonal issues popped up between those 120 people over the course of those ten days.

Put yourself in their shoes. They're excited and expectant because they know God has spoken, and that He has something for them. All they have to do is "tarry" for a "few days." I'm sure their zeal and excitement carried them through the first day or two. But then a third day passed. And a fourth. Then five days, and nothing. Then six. Still zip. Then a week. Then more than a week. Then way more than a week. Had they missed it? Had they misinterpreted what the Lord had said? Was it the new guy's fault—after all he had only come to Jesus a few days ago? Maybe it's because of that one woman who was off-key every time she sang? Were tongues perhaps no longer for today? Was it because someone's skirt was too short or hair was too long?

Churches of fewer people have split over less important things than contending for a promise of God and it seemingly not all going according to schedule.

In those ten days leading up to Pentecost, there was every opportunity to give place to finger-pointing, name-calling, theological disputes, style differences, discord, and division. But those 120 champions chose to remain of one accord. They chose to remain focused on the promise as opposed to blaming one another for why it had not yet come to pass. They chose the power of unity. And Heaven exploded in their midst!

> ## Unity does not mean total agreement all the time.

To achieve true Kingdom unity and begin to unlock this realm of power, we have to understand something crucial. We have to get that "unity" does not mean complete and total agreement on every topic, issue, and scriptural interpretation. The key to unity in the church is not thinking and believing exactly alike on all things at all times. The key to unity is choosing to continue on in relationship, specifically when there is a disagreement.

Amos 3:3 is sometimes referred to as the "church split" Scripture because it's often the passage that's cited by one or both sides as the reason they need to leave in a huff—and usually a wake of devastation. It asks the question of how two can walk together if they are not in agreement. The first thing that it's important to note is that this Scripture is a question, not a statement.

Amos 3:3 does not say that if there is a lack of agreement there cannot be cooperation, harmony, or unity. Just the opposite. It asks *how* can two walk together when there is a lack of agreement on something. The answer? The character and nature of Christ within our born-again spirits. After all, haven't each of us at times done or said or thought something that Jesus was not in agreement with, and yet He continued walking with, loving and mentoring us. Never compromising truth, but also never forsaking or abandoning us. His character and nature—His image in which we are made—is the answer to how we embrace unity in the midst of disagreement.

Let's go back to the Upper Room in Acts 2 for a minute. We already talked about how over the course of those way-more-than-a-few days the 120 believers more than likely had lots of opportunities to get upset, frustrated, or even angry with one another. They certainly had multiple chances to disagree and divide. But they chose not to. What was their secret? It's right there in Acts 2 verse 1 of the classic King James Version of the Bible when it says they were of *"one accord."* That word *accord* in the Greek is made of two root words. One means "same place and same time." The other means "passion." So the key to staying together in the same "place" at the same "time," *especially* when there are opportunities for disagreement, offense, discord, and division, is to have the same passion—the Lord. Those 120 champions were able to stay the course in unity because they were more focused on Him than they were on anything else.

Agreeing that Jesus is Lord is more than enough common ground for any of His children to meet upon. When we are more in love with Him than we are with being right, it becomes very easy to maintain unity, even when there are differences of opinion. And that unity opens up realms of power just like at Pentecost. Why do you think the enemy works so hard to get us to turn on one another?

UNITY DRAWS GOD'S BLESSING AND POWER

One of the ministries I lead is called Men on the Frontlines. Its focus is to help men realize who they are as sons of God, and all that they've been empowered with to be difference-makers and solution-bringers in every sphere of influence they're operating in and are called to.

I clearly remember the encounter I had with the Lord when He gave me this ministry as well as the strategy to birth it by initially creating connection and community among men through online and streaming media. The first year and a half was challenging, but many lessons were learned and much ground was gained. Then, at just the right time, God showed me just the right ally to take the reach and influence of Men on the Frontlines to the next level.

When Brad Carter agreed to be part of Men on the Frontlines, he brought different skills and experiences to the ministry. His strong apostolic gifting was a great addition to my prophetic orientation. But even more, I now see that Brad added into the mix a sense of brotherhood. Brad and I had been friends for years. We had been through thick and thin together. We were allies. We had a covenant sense of unity.

When Brad joined Men on the Frontlines, God commanded a blessing in our midst, and the ministry expanded to an international reach. We were not only creating lots of online content, we were now doing men's conferences, events, and retreats throughout the USA and overseas. Man after man told us that they had never experienced men's ministry like this. They had never felt so equipped and empowered. Brad and I know we're good at what we do, but we are well aware that it's God's commanded blessing in our midst that makes our Men on the Frontlines events special.

After about a year of Brad and I working together, God brought us another ally. It was a similar story with Ben Hughes. Ben has different skills and anointings from Brad and I; and what knitted us together was a sense of Holy Spirit-orchestrated brotherhood and unity. Despite being a seasoned and experienced revivalist who had stewarded a major move of God in Australia, Ben came to one of our Men on the Frontlines events simply to serve and be with the guys. Both Brad and I felt a strong connection with Ben, and the three of us have co-labored together on our Men on the Frontlines events ever since.

We have seen God move powerfully in our midst again and again and again. Men have been restored. Wounds have been healed. Marriages have been mended. Souls have been saved. Businesses have been multiplied and increased. Men have not only become empowered, they have become moves of God in their families, communities, cities, and regions.

Brad, Ben, and I rarely all agree on everything, but we know we are in this together with and for Jesus, as well as with and for the men we are blessed to fellowship with, minister to, and empower. The choice Ben, Brad, and I have made to be in unity has propelled Men on the Frontlines higher than any of us could have carried it on our own.

ACTIVATE THE POWER OF UNITY

God loves unity. God responds to unity. God moves powerfully in the midst of unity—because He is all about relationship. Choosing to be in relationship is choosing to bring Heaven to earth. That is why unity is so powerful. And why the enemy hates it so much. The enemy knows we are more powerful together than apart. We need to wake up to this too.

The following keys will help you begin to put the power of unity to work in your life.

1. Watch out for the accuser (Revelation 12:10).

If the enemy can't get us to separate from God, he will work overtime to get us to separate from one another. This usually begins with fault-finding and accusations. Finger-pointing is not a ministry. And when it comes to policing the Body of Christ, that is almost always better left to the Holy Spirit.

Look to the example of Jesus Himself. In John 1 when Nathaniel is told that the Messiah has come and He is from Nazareth, Nathaniel has nothing good to say about the whole situation (see John 1:45-46). Yet when Jesus encounters Nathaniel, He does not find fault with him. Jesus doesn't accuse Nathaniel of being a "jerk," or a "guy with an attitude problem," or a "negative pain-in-the-rear." He easily could have, but instead Jesus refers to Nathaniel as an Israelite *"in whom there is no deceit"* (John 1:47 NASB). Jesus does not accuse Nathaniel of his shortcomings, He focuses on and speaks to the best aspect of who he is—a man who tells you what is on his mind. Choosing to see the best in someone is a huge key to unlocking the power of unity.

2. Realize God loves diversity.

In the Old Testament, God had twelve tribes. In the New Testament, He started out with twelve disciples. They had different natures, personalities, backgrounds, and giftings. Differences are not bad—including differences of opinion. God is okay with diversity. He didn't just make one tree or flower or fish or dog. He made a diversity of each of them. Actually, He made a diversity of everything. He is good with diversity, but He does not like division. Evangelists are passionate about evangelism. Worshippers love to worship. Pastors love to listen and support. Teachers love to educate and disciple. Apostles love to build. Prophets love to cast vision. Those are all different giftings and callings. And they are all good.

We can celebrate and champion the focus of another without giving up what we're called to and are passionate about. We can find the members of our tribe and run with them, without pointing fingers at another tribe and telling them they're doing it wrong. If the hands told the liver it needed to be just like them, the body would shut down pretty quickly because there would no longer be the God-created organ to remove toxins. Division is toxic and can shut down the Body of Christ. Just because someone has a different calling, gift, focus, or revelation from you does not mean they are wrong (or a Jezebel, anti-Christ, deceiver, heretic, or false prophet).

3. Gather together—especially when you might not want to.

In Hebrews 10:25 we are told not to forsake gathering together. Part of the reason for this, we are told in that same passage, is because when we are in unity we can motivate and encourage one another. But notice that the Scripture does not just say for us to gather together, it specifically instructs us not to *forsake* gathering together. In other words, when you are about to forsake it because your feelings are hurt or you didn't get your way or someone else was asked to lead the prayer or bring the message, that is the exact time *not* to quit fellowshipping. That is the time to choose to be in unity.

To unlock the power of unity in our lives, we can't be loners. So it is key that you find a church, Bible study, or men's or women's group. And that you commit to being a member of it. That doesn't mean you will never move on from that group, it means you commit to working through any issues in unity until a day you do feel God calling you to a new place. When that happens, you will move on in love and with honor, not in a huff and spewing all that was wrong with those people.

4. Disagree without dishonoring or dividing.

No matter how great your church or group is, you are going to have disagreements. I have walked with the core leadership of our ministry for almost twenty years. We have not always agreed. We have had differences of opinion on passages of Scripture, approaches to situations, and even on budget and financial issues. But what we have never disagreed on is that we are all in this together. When we have a disagreement we do not dishonor, and we do not divide, because we know we are stronger together than apart and that God will command His blessing in our midst and give us wisdom if we continue to walk together. He has never failed to do so. By choosing unity, we are not weakened by disagreements, we are actually strengthened in our resolve to walk as one.

So when disagreements come up—and they will—don't see them as problems, see them as opportunities. Don't divide over them. And definitely do not speak ill of one another. You are simply having a disagreement. Intentionally stay the course. Process through the disagreements. Be willing to hear one another's hearts. Choose unity and watch God move in your midst.

5. Refuse offense.

Few things bring division as quickly as offense. That is because offense creates "a fence." It causes a hardening of the heart that creates an emotional boundary between us and someone else because of something they said or did. Offense gives our carnal nature a reason to rationalize a victim mentality so that we feel justified in withdrawing. Offense creates division based on selfishness and self-protection. The key to refusing offense is to remember that offense is taken not given. It is a choice.

If someone does something offensive, you do not have to take offense. Instead you can go to the person and process through it. I have helped many members of our team process through these type of situations, and we have always grown closer and stronger when we were willing to hear one another and grow together. The few times that didn't occur was in the rare instance when someone wasn't willing to let go of the offense.

6. Pray for those with whom you disagree.

When disagreements occur, especially ones you are considering dividing over, take the time to pray for the person or people you disagree with. This is especially important when you feel the need to create a temporary boundary to feel safe or so healing can occur. Prayer will help keep you from separating in the spirit. Seek God's heart for the "other side." Ask Him to help you see the good in them, as well as any root issues you can pray into on their behalf. And remember that you are praying for them. You are not praying self-righteous, God-get-them prayers. Being willing to pray for those you do not agree with is an act of unity. It connects you with God. It helps you to see others as He sees them. And it is a declaration in the spirit that even if for a moment, or a season, you are separate from them, you choose not to be divided.

7. You're not called to walk with everyone.

It's okay if there are those with whom you don't connect. You're not called to be in unity with everyone. Just realize you are also not called to be against anyone. Find your tribe. Run with them. Be committed to unity with them. And as for those you're not called to run with, it's okay if you disagree with their focus. You already decided it wasn't for you anyway. So don't spend time attacking them or complaining about them to others—whether that is in person, online, on the phone, or any other way. When you do that, you are not helping God, you're in league with the accuser of the brethren.

– 5 –

Power of
Repentance

...Repent, for the kingdom

of heaven is at hand

(Matthew 4:17 NASB).

IF you've accepted Jesus Christ as your Lord and Savior, you already have an inherent understanding of the massive power of repentance, because it has changed your life. What you may not actually understand, however, is what repentance truly is and the power it has to change our world.

Let's start by talking about what repentance is not.

Too many Christians think that to repent means to hang our head in shame and feel really, really bad about our sins That is not what repentance is at all. When Jesus came and invited us to repent (see Matthew 4:17), He was *not* saying, "I am here to make you feel lousy." Our Savior does not traffic in shame and condemnation (see Romans 8:1). He is all about light in the darkness. His goal has never been to mire us in guilt over our sins, it has always been to set us free from them.

When Jesus preached and said in Matthew 4:17 (NKJV), *"Repent, for the kingdom of heaven is at hand,"* He was not pointing a finger. He was presenting us with an alternative. A different way, a better way. His invitation for us to repent is not about who we've been and what we've done wrong, His invitation for us to repent is all about the opportunity to realize that through Him the Kingdom of Heaven is at hand—and we can grab hold of it.

Repentance is not about looking at what we have done wrong and feeling bad about it. Repentance is about looking at Jesus and realizing there is a whole different way of living.

Yes, of course, we need to understand that we are sinners and need a Savior. That is a must. But it is the gift of conviction from the Holy Spirit that brings the awareness of sin (see John 16:7-8). Repentance is all about the realization that we have a Savior, that He has provided a better way, and because of that realization we then choose to say yes to His far superior and much more powerful way of living in this world.

One other thing we often hear about repentance is that it means to turn away from sin. That is actually the result of repentance, not the act of repentance. Turning from sin is a huge blessing that comes along with the power of repentance. But technically repentance is not so much turning from sin as it is turning from how you have thought about sin and rebellion and carnality and selfishness of every kind. When the Holy Spirit helps you see how truly limiting, dangerous, and destructive all the traps, lies, and lures of sin and rebellion are, the power of repentance helps you change your mind about their supposed allure. In the realization that sin, rebellion, and selfishness lead to nothing but bondage and destruction, you then choose to turn away from them. Praise God!

REPENTANCE MEANS TO THINK DIFFERENTLY

The real power in repentance is to change how we think about pretty much everything. That is actually what *repentance* means. The Greek word used for *repentance* in the New Testament is *metanoeo,* which means "to think differently; i.e., reconsider."

One of the very first things the power of repentance helps us to think differently about is Jesus.

In Matthew 16:13 (NLT), Jesus asked the disciples, *"Who do people say that the Son of Man is?"* Their response was to share the contemporary views of how Jesus was thought of in that day. A prophet, a reincarnation of Elijah or Jeremiah, and other thoughts along those lines. But then Jesus asked, *"But who do **you** say I am?"* (Matthew 16:15 NLT). In that moment, Peter gets a download from Heaven and declares that Jesus is much more than a prophet, teacher, wise man, or a religious leader. Peter declares that Jesus is the Messiah, the Son of the Living

God (see Matthew 16:16). Peter is able to see things from the perspective of Heaven and think differently from the rest of the world about who Jesus is. That is the power of repentance—a revelatory moment of divine insight that allows us to see things differently, and begin to make different choices.

If you read the first chapter of this book, you know a bit of my story. For almost four decades my take on Jesus was that He was little more than a myth or a legend. Maybe, I thought, He was some kind of guru or teacher; but just as likely, if He ever even really existed, I figured He was a con man as much as a holy man. If I gave it any real thought at all, I figured that Jesus and Christianity were probably just another set of fairy tales.

But then one day, outside my cabin in the woods of Northwest Montana, that all changed. All of a sudden I thought *very* differently about Jesus. I reconsidered everything about Him. I knew He was real. I knew He loved me. I knew He was God. I knew He was my Savior. I knew I very much needed Him. And I knew that I wanted Him to be Lord of my life. That change of mind and heart. That change of perspective. That change of thinking. That is the power of repentance. It changed everything for me. And continues to. The power of repentance starts with changing how we think about Jesus. But it doesn't end there.

REPENTANCE CHANGES EVERYTHING

Each of us has had a moment when the power of repentance gave us the ability to think differently about Jesus. Maybe like me, you mocked or dismissed Him. Or perhaps you grew up in a Christian family but thought of Jesus as your mom's or dad's God or Savior, not yours. Or perhaps you were somewhere in between. But a day came when all of a sudden you knew who Jesus was, what He had done, why He had done it, and how desperately you wanted and needed Him. In that realization, you chose to turn from the way you had been living and began to live with and for Jesus. That is the power of repentance. The ability to see something from God's perspective, know it is true, and turn away from the lies of the world and the enemy that have limited or trapped you in the past.

Repentance empowers us to think differently about everything. It brings a supernatural ability to change our minds so we can embrace a divine opportunity in Christ to change our lives. The power of repentance is the power to align with the truth of God so that the lies of the enemy and the draws of the flesh no longer tempt us or control us.

There is a reason the first word of Jesus's public ministry here on earth was, *"Repent"* (see Matthew 4:17). He was inviting us to reconsider everything. Why? Because the Kingdom of Heaven was now at hand. There was now a better way to grab hold of Him. Jesus had come to change everything; but He knew for us to walk in all He was making available, we would first need to change the way we thought. As we did, we would choose to turn from the paths that we had been on and start to walk with Him. As our Savior, yes. But also as our Lord. Which means we would reconsider anything in our minds, hearts, or lives that did not align with His will, ways, and truth so that we could choose to turn from those things, and turn to Him. The power of repentance helps us do this.

First the power of repentance changes us. It helps us think differently. Think Kingdom. Think truth. It helps us avoid or escape the lies, lures, traps, and temptations of the enemy, because we now see them for what they are. And we choose to go a different way. That then begins to change the lives of those around us.

Consider the woman who is going to have an abortion. What is she thinking? Perhaps that she does not have the financial means to raise a child. Or maybe that she is not ready or able to handle such a big responsibility. She most definitely isn't thinking about the "fetus" as a blessed life brought forth by God for a divine purpose on earth. What is the solution? *Repent!* All of a sudden she stops thinking about her challenges and begins to think about what would be best for the baby. Now she not only reconsiders aborting the child, but starts to think about putting the baby up for adoption. The power of repentance changes how she sees her situation, saves the life of a child, and perhaps even helps fulfill the dreams of a previously barren couple who wanted to start a family of their own.

Consider the churchgoer who thinks tithes and offerings are nothing but an outdated Old Testament custom used to pry money from his wallet. The solution? *Repent!* Change from thinking about the weekly offering at church as something to be avoided, and see it for the Kingdom opportunity it is to be a blessing and to be blessed. When that parishioner grabs hold of the power of repentance he not only begins to unlock a realm of financial increase in his own life, but he becomes part of the Kingdom works his church is doing to feed the poor, buy books for inner-city libraries, and launch mission trips to preach the Gospel in the nations. The eternal rewards for all of that are now also unto his account in Heaven. His blessings increase on earth and in the life to come. Plus the lives of many others are changed by the work he is now sowing into. All because of the power of repentance.

Consider the believer who has never seen a miracle so isn't sure they still happen. The answer? *Repent!* She reconsiders. Perhaps, she thinks, the reason she has never seen a miracle is simply because she has never been willing to believe for one. As she grabs hold of the power of repentance, her thinking changes. She realizes that since Jesus is the same yesterday, today, and forever and His Word is eternally true, then so must be the truth that she is to heal the sick, cast out demons, and raise the dead! She becomes a believer who works miracles. The lame walk, the blind see, the deaf hear, backs are healed, and legs grow out. All because of the power of repentance.

Consider the husband who is committing adultery. At some point he foolishly chose to think of cheating on his wife as an option to working on his marriage. Instead of being open, honest, and doing the hard work to mend his covenant relationship, he chose to indulge his flesh. Perhaps he told himself it was no big deal, and that his wife would never know. Or maybe he figured it was his right because his needs weren't being met at home. The answer? *Repent!* He needs to change how he thinks about it all. He needs to stop focusing on escaping the issues in his marriage because he doesn't know how to address them, and realize that the Kingdom of Heaven is at hand. As he does, he will understand that he has the opportunity to turn away from sin and bring healing to his marriage—changing his life, and the lives of his wife, children, and family.

REPENTANCE CAN EVEN CHANGE NATIONS

We have seen how the power of repentance can totally change things in our lives, as well as in the lives of others. But it can also change things on earth—including our nations. Look at Second Chronicles 7:14 (NKJV):

> *If My people who are called by My name will humble them-selves, and pray and seek My face, and turn from their wicked ways, then I will hear from heaven, and will forgive their sin and heal their land.*

This Scripture is within the context of God revealing how His people can shift things on earth when there are times of drought, disease, and devastation. All it takes is the power of repentance. When there is darkness and difficulty in our land, it is usually because we have tried to make our own way and our own rules. We have made compromises. We have sinned and turned from God.

But if we are now willing to approach things differently, that can all change. If we are willing to humble ourselves, seek God, embrace His will, and then turn away from any of our wicked ways it will bring forth a divine response. In other words, when we change how we think about the whole situation and embrace God's way of approaching things, He will respond and heal the land.

It is not up to conservatives or liberals. It is not up to a certain politician or leader. It is up to us as God's people. We can initiate great change in our nations through the power of repentance.

ACTIVATE THE POWER OF REPENTANCE

The key to activating the power of repentance is to be willing to "change your mind." So to begin opening this realm of power, let the Lord know you desire to see things and think about things as He does.

1. Ask the Holy Spirit to show you where you need to repent.

We don't always know where we have bought into a lie of the enemy, our flesh, or even of faulty theology until the Lord reveals it to us. Ask Holy Spirit to search your heart and mind. Invite Him to shine a light on any deception or wrong way of thinking.

2. Read your Bible every day.

Reading your Bible every day is not legalism, religion, or even a "rule" you must obey. This is recognizing that God has given us an amazing tool and resource. We would be foolish not to utilize it each and every day. The Word of God is the greatest source of wisdom and truth available. It reveals God's heart and lets us know what He thinks about every situation. According to Hebrews 4:12, your Bible is way more than simply print on a page. It is active and alive. So when you interact with your Bible, it actually interacts with you. Or, as I heard a preacher say years ago, "When you read your Bible, it reads you!"

The Word of God searches your heart and mind. It shows where your thoughts are out of sync with God's thoughts. It reveals where you have given in to compromise or believed a lie. God's Word can actually examine your motives and intentions to reveal where you need the power of repentance to help change your mind.

3. When you see the truth, turn from the lie.

The power of repentance helps you reconsider your thoughts, choices, and actions. It empowers you to see where you have been out of alignment with God's truth, and change your mind so you are in agreement with the Kingdom of Heaven. But it does not end there. Remember that there is a result that always comes with true repentance—turning away from the error, deception, and sin. When you truly repent and truly change your mind, you will also change your behavior. After all, we are not only to know God's truth, we are to live from it (see James 1:22).

– 6 –

Power to Shift Atmospheres

And He got up and rebuked the
wind and said to the sea, "Hush,
be still." And the wind died down
and it became perfectly calm
(Mark 4:39 NASB).

IN Mark 4:39, Jesus spoke to the storm, and the wind and waves became calm. He shifted the atmosphere. We see it clearly, and have no problem believing that He could do that. But what about us? The very next thing Jesus says indicates that He wants us to wake up to the reality that when we walk with Him we have the power to shift atmospheres too.

Let's look a bit closer at what was happening in this passage of Scripture (see Mark 4:35-40). Jesus and His disciples are heading from one side of the lake to the other. They get in a boat and start their journey. Jesus lays down in the back, and falls asleep. Then at some point along the way a fierce storm kicks up. The winds get stronger and stronger. The waves get higher and higher until the sea is crashing over the gunwales and filling the boat. The disciples are frantic. They shout at Jesus to wake Him up. He rebukes the storm, and a great calm comes forth. But then He asks the disciples two key questions. First, *"Why are you afraid?"* And second, *"Do you still have no faith?"*

Remember that Jesus was not only Messiah, He was also Mentor. He doesn't ask questions of the disciples—or us, for that matter—because He is lacking knowledge. He asks them questions to help them learn. He is their Rabbi. He is discipling them. He is mentoring them on how to walk with God on earth. He is always revealing what that looks like, so they can learn to walk in what He is modeling to them. After all, that was His invitation to the disciples when He said, *"Come, follow me"* (Matthew 4:19 NLT).

This is also His invitation to each of us. Not only to believe in Him, but to walk with Him in that belief. To follow Him. To learn to do what He did (see John 14:12). Because He knew that one day they, and we, would be the Body of Christ on earth—an expression of the Kingdom that puts the reality of our heavenly Father on display in a variety of ways.

When Jesus asked the disciples why they were afraid in the storm, He was not belittling them. He wanted them to consider why they let their circumstances so impact their outlook. Yes, a storm had kicked up. And yes, it was fierce. But didn't they have the word of the Lord that they were headed to the other side of the lake? Why was their fear of the storm greater than their trust in His promise? That's what He was asking them.

His next question, *"Do you still have no faith?"* was about why they feared the storm at all. He wasn't asking about their faith in Him. It's clear they had faith in Jesus. After all, when they realized how serious the storm was, the first thing they did was cry out to Him for help. They had great faith in Him. What they didn't have any faith in was that *they* could have done something to address the situation. That's what Jesus was getting at. Why, after all He had shared with them, taught them, modeled to them, and mentored them in, had they not yet realized that when they have a promise from God, they also have the authority to see that promise come forth?

Jesus calmed the storm because that is who He is and what He does. He is Savior. He is all about rescuing us from our own limitations. But He is also about getting us past those limitations so we can live in the realms of power He has opened up for us. So way more than having the disciples see Him calm the storm, Jesus wanted them to "see" that they could have done it. He wanted them to realize that because they were walking with Him, they could have shifted the atmosphere.

As Christians, we are not to be influenced or affected by atmospheres here on earth. Just the opposite, actually. We are empowered to affect and influence them. The Lord gave me a powerful revelation of this early on in my walk with Him.

A LESSON AT 35,000 FEET

I was on a commercial airline flight heading home from the East Coast after a very fruitful weekend of ministry. I'd poured out multiple sessions a day for several days in a row. We went from morning to evening, and often late into the night. Needless to say, I was tired. For the first bit of my flight back to Phoenix I caught up on some work. After a little while my eyes were getting weary, so I closed the computer, and cued up a worship music playlist. My plan was to spend some quiet time with the Lord, and maybe even sleep for an hour or so.

Just as I was getting comfortable in my seat, we hit some heavy turbulence. After quite a few big bumps, the pilot announced over the intercom that the flight attendants would need to suspend the food and beverage service and strap into their seats. He let us know we would be flying through rough air for the next twenty minutes or so.

I am not a nervous flyer, but I do not like heavy turbulence. As the shaking began to increase, I spoke to God about it. "Lord, I was really looking forward to some quiet time with You. Could You please do something about all the bumping and shaking?"

His reply was gentle and encouraging, but it also took me by surprise. *You do it,* He said.

In that instant He brought to mind the same passage of Scripture we started this chapter with—when He stood in the boat and commanded the storm to be still. He reminded me that as a believer I was called and empowered to do the works that He did (see John 14:12). Eyes closed, worship music playing in my headphones, and being bounced around by all that turbulence, I started to think, *Well, because Jesus is the same yesterday, today and forever, and He is with us everywhere we go, it makes sense that what worked at sea level for Him, should work at cruising altitude with Him.*

At the leading of the Holy Spirit, I began to pray. I quietly spoke to the storm of the air, commanding the waves of wind that were buffeting the plane to "Be still!"

Almost immediately the rough air smoothed. Within a moment or two, the pilot came back on the intercom and announced in a somewhat surprised tone that the turbulence had suddenly dissipated. He let the flight attendants know it was now safe to get up and resume cabin service. The atmosphere had shifted!

Our God is an Atmosphere Shifter, and so are we.

As I reflect back on this experience all these years later, I find it curious that it took a nudge from the Lord for me to step out and deal with the turbulence. Of course the power and authority of God can shift atmospheres on earth. The Bible begins with a display of that exact thing:

> The earth was without form, and void; and darkness was on the face of the deep. And the Spirit of God was hovering over the face of the waters. Then God said, "Let there be light"; and there was light (Genesis 1:2-3 NKJV).

The first thing God shows us through His Word is that He is an atmosphere shifter. There was darkness. He shifted it to light. There was void,

He spends verses 4 through 25 of Genesis 1 shifting that atmosphere of formlessness by bringing forth all of creation. Then in verses 26 to 28, He makes us in His image, and empowers us to steward His creation in His deputized authority. We are made in the very likeness of He who is the Shifter of Atmospheres. Is it any wonder that in Him, with Him and for Him, we have the power to shift atmospheres, as well?

In the New Testament, Jesus reminds us of something very similar. When He shares with the disciples how to pray in Matthew 6:9-10 (NASB), He says to them:

> *Pray, then, in this way:*
> *"Our Father, who is in heaven,*
> *Hallowed be Your name.*
> *Your kingdom come.*
> *Your will be done,*
> ***On earth as it is in heaven."***

Jesus was helping the disciples see that when they walk with the Father through the gift of His Son, they have the ability—through His deputized authority and power—to shift atmospheres. Anywhere they see it not yet on earth as it is in Heaven, they are to pray and believe for it to shift. It's the same for anything that would stand in the way of His promises coming forth—we are to shift that atmosphere.

On earth as it is in heaven.

ANY AND ALL ATMOSPHERES, ANYWHERE YOU GO

The power to shift atmospheres that Jesus has opened to us is not only about speaking to storms. It is, as we see in Scripture, about co-laboring with our Father in Heaven as His dominion stewards on earth to see any atmosphere that is not in line with Kingdom truth, shift from dark to light. We are empowered in Christ to shift the atmosphere of sickness and disease to an atmosphere of health, vigor, and vitality (see Mark 16:18). Atmospheres of lack can be shifted to atmospheres of abundance (see Philippians 4:19). Heavy atmospheres of oppression can be shifted to freedom (see Acts 10:38). Mourning can be shifted to joy (see Isaiah 61:3). Even death can be shifted to life (see Acts 20:9-10).

Wherever the enemy has established an atmosphere of any kind of "darkness," we have the power to shift that to "light" (see Luke 10:19). Any atmosphere that Jesus has shifted for us, we can shift on earth to His glory. We are commissioned by Him to freely give to others what He has freely given to us (see Matthew 10:8). We can do this in our own lives, in the lives of others, at work, in our family and relationships, even in our neighborhoods, cities, and nations. Glory to God!

Let me share one more story about how the Lord mentored me in shifting the atmosphere of an entire city.

About ten years ago, through my first open-eyed angelic encounter, the Lord called me to Europe. Specifically a key region of Eastern Europe.

I had done quite a bit of ministry and missions into the nations prior to this call. I was used to seeing great fruit come forth everywhere we went—from Ethiopia and Mongolia to Thailand, Cambodia and Singapore. On most overseas trips we regularly saw the Lord work through us to heal, do miracles, lead many to salvation, and give us great favor with the lost and hurting.

My first trip into Eastern Europe was very different. No one would talk to me on the streets. If I said hello, people completely ignored me and hurried in the other direction. It was the same when I tried to talk to waiters and waitresses, or people in shops. No one wanted to talk. No one was willing to let me pray for them. No one wanted to interact or connect. Everyone was so guarded. They all wanted to be left alone.

I tried to get locals to go on outreach with me, but they told me that there was no point. They said only drunks or crazy people talk to strangers on the street or in shops, so there was no way people would be willing to stop for a conversation. On top of this cultural roadblock, there was also a tangible spiritual atmosphere of heaviness and oppression hanging over the region from decades of Soviet occupation and domination.

It was pretty discouraging; but I knew that if the Lord had called me to this place, He must have a plan. I might have been surprised by how shut down the area seemed to be, but I knew the Lord wasn't. So I went into prayer to seek His heart.

The plan He gave me was simple. He invited me to launch a "smile ministry." He asked me to go out onto the streets, into the shops, parks, and public places and simply walk, pray, and whenever I could catch someone's eye, even if only for a moment, smile at them. He invited me to fill my thoughts, my heart, and my eyes with Him, and then intentionally release that out to everyone I could through a smile. A warm, kind, caring smile. A Jesus smile.

So that's what I did. Every day. Sometimes for hours at a time.

I also shared the vision of the "smile ministry" in every church where I preached and ministered, inviting others to join me in this "outreach" as they went about their days.

It was that simple. Smile. And it worked.

Over time, the entire atmosphere of the city changed. From dark and dour. To light and joyful. From those first few days out on the streets when people couldn't get away from me fast enough. To us having teams throughout the city and in the parks ministering to people. There were even days when folks lined up so we could pray for them, prophesy over them, and encourage them.

The shift didn't happen in a day. It didn't happen in a week, a month, or even a year. But it happened. Gradually at first. And then more and more over time. I remember one day walking the streets of that wonderful city when the Lord spoke to me nearly audibly, *Look around.* I was on one of the main downtown boulevards. I stopped and did exactly as He asked. I slowly turned in a semi-circle taking in the streets, the park, the shops. Everywhere I looked I saw people walking and talking, laughing, and smiling. It had been almost six years since my first trip, and it looked and felt so very different. The atmosphere had shifted.

ACTIVATE THE POWER TO SHIFT ATMOSPHERES

There is an old saying that a Christian is much more than a thermometer. We are more like thermostats. We not only can measure the temperature of a room, we can change it. It's the same with atmospheres. We can do more than discern them, we can shift them. Any atmosphere. Anywhere. Any time.

Here are several keys to help you get activated in the power to shift atmospheres.

1. Pay attention.

The first step to shifting an atmosphere is knowing that it needs shifting. Be on the lookout for indications that you are in the midst of an atmosphere that is not what God intended for that person, place, or situation.

2. Know who you are and who you walk with.

Often when we encounter an atmosphere that needs shifting we are tempted to check out. Oppressive and demonic atmospheres can be overwhelming. Especially if they are long-established negative atmospheres in regions, cities, or families. They feel immovable and overwhelming. We are tempted to disengage and accept them because in ourselves we feel powerless. "It's always been that way." "They'll never change." "I can't wait to get out of here." Those types of thoughts are all indications that you are in an atmosphere that needs shifting. You are not powerless. You are a dominion steward on earth. You are made in the image of the Genesis 1 Changer of Atmospheres Himself. You walk with the Lord Almighty and He has escorted you into this atmosphere to shift it. You may be surprised by the atmosphere, but He is not. He has a great plan for how you can shift things. Ask Him.

3. Bind and loose.

In Matthew 16:19, Jesus let His disciples know that we have the power to bind on earth what has been bound in Heaven. We also have the power in Him to loose into the earth from Heaven. When you encounter an atmosphere that is not on earth as it is in Heaven, bind that atmosphere. Then loose what the heavenly atmosphere is. Years ago when I was in a certain city I sensed a very oppressive atmosphere of depression and addiction. Pastors in the region confirmed to me that both of those were huge issues in that area. That is not on earth as it is in Heaven. So for the first few days that I was in that city, I bound the darkness and oppression of depression and addiction while also loosing the light of freedom and joy into the area. During my time there we saw many people set free from alcohol and drug addiction, while also having their joy restored.

4. Send forth the Word.

Isaiah 55:11 says that God's Word never returns void, and that it always bears fruit. When you read further on in that passage, it is clear that God's proclaimed Word shifts atmospheres into joy and peace; and it even shifts regions into greater fruitfulness. In Matthew 8 we see the example of Jesus sending forth the Word and the Roman Centurion's servant is healed miles away. God's Word is so powerful that when you send it forth with faith and intention, you do not even have to be in a region or with a person to see an atmosphere shift.

5. Praise and worship.

Heaven is filled with 24-7 worship of the King (see Revelation 4:8-11). When we worship God here on earth we are bringing Heaven's atmosphere into this realm. That shifts things. According to Isaiah 61:3, praising God can shift atmospheres of heaviness to joy and gladness. We see a great example of this in Acts 16:16-34 when Paul and Silas are in prison. Instead of murmuring or complaining about their situation, they choose to worship the Lord. They see a great shift from captivity to freedom. And not just for them. All the prison doors are flung wide, every prisoner is released, the jailer is saved, and a great revival breaks out at the jailer's home. Praise and worship shifts the atmosphere.

6. Lift up a shout.

If the enemy seems to have a stronghold in your life, family, workplace, city, or nation, release a shout of victory to tear that stronghold down and shift the atmosphere. In Matthew 27:50 we see Jesus do this exact thing. As He hung on the Cross He cried out with a *"loud voice."* That shout was the triumphant roar of the Lion of Judah. The enemy was defeated, and the shekinah glory of God was released from the Temple to go out and cover the earth. Talk about an atmosphere shift! We see something similar in Joshua 6. When the enemy was occupying territory meant for the people of God, the Lord told Joshua and the Israelites to blow the trumpets and release a *"Shout!"* (see Joshua 6:16 NASB). When they did, the fortifications of the enemy crumbled. The atmosphere shifted from the enemy holding the land to the people of God occupying the territory.

7. Speak to the storms.

When in doubt, do what Jesus did. Always a great idea! Never hesitate to speak to any storm and simply command it to, "Be still!" This can be especially effective with what I call "storm patterns." I have often seen these in families and even churches—negative atmospheres that seem well established and often occur at every meeting, gathering, or event. Before the next get-together, take authority over those storm patterns. Silence them. Command them to be still. Don't forget to also loose and declare the heavenly atmosphere into those gatherings. The more often you do this, the greater the shift you will see.

– 7 –

Power of Tongues

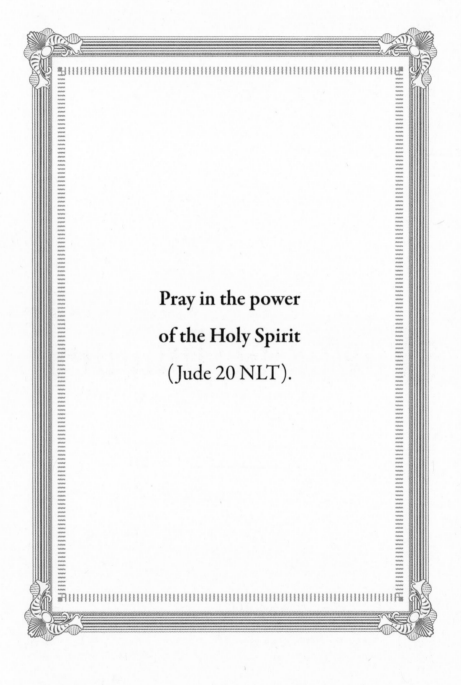

Pray in the power
of the Holy Spirit
(Jude 20 NLT).

THERE'S a reason the apostle Paul told the church of Corinth that he wished they all prayed in tongues (see 1 Corinthians 14:5). It's because he knew from firsthand experience the realm of power it opens up for believers (see 1 Corinthians 14:18).

What we commonly refer to as "tongues" is one of the gifts of the Holy Spirit (see 1 Corinthians 12:4-10). Different translations, refer to this gift in different ways. The Amplified Bible simply says, *"tongues."* The New American Standard Bible translates it as *"various kinds of tongues."* The King James Bible lists it as *"diverse tongues."* My personal favorite is The Passion Translation that says, *"the gift of speaking different kinds of tongues."* I like that one best because it comes right out and calls tongues a gift while also pointing out that there are different facets to this power-packed blessing.

Through the gift of tongues, the Holy Spirit supernaturally empowers us to speak languages beyond our natural ability. One aspect of this is to all-of-a-sudden be able to speak earthly languages without having studied or learned them. Another is to speak a heavenly language that unlocks multiple realms of divine power in our lives.

A SUPERNATURAL WITNESS OF OUR SUPERNATURAL GOD

Acts 2:4-12 is probably the clearest example of how the Holy Spirit can empower us through the gift of tongues to supernaturally speak in an earthly language we had not previously known. As soon as the believers in the Upper Room were filled with the Holy Spirit, they went out on the streets to bear witness of Jesus Christ. They were all Galileans, but they began speaking in the languages and dialects of every tourist, visitor, and immigrant who were in the city and had come running to see what the roar, wind, and fire of Pentecost had been about.

There were Iranians, Syrians, Turks, Iraqis, Judeans, Libyans, Egyptians, Cretans, Arabs, and travelers from throughout the Roman Empire and Asia. Thousands of people were present. Each and every one of them heard testimony of the reality of Jesus and His mighty wonders *in their own language*. Acts 2:12 says that they were all astonished and amazed by this supernatural phenomenon. And in the end, because they heard the Word of the Lord in their native tongues, thousands came into a saving knowledge of Jesus as the Messiah.

That's the purpose of this facet of the gift of tongues—to be a sign and a wonder that empowers us to quite literally speak to people where they are (and where they're from) in their native language about the reality of Jesus. It is a supernatural witness of our supernatural God.

My experience with this aspect of the power of tongues is that there are times you're aware it's happening, and other times you have no idea.

SOMETIMES ALL YOU HAVE TO DO IS ASK

For years I led power evangelism schools and short-term missions trips in Pattaya, Thailand—an international destination for sex tourism. Believers would join us from all around the world, and we would teach them how to move in miracles by sharing the extreme love of Jesus in some truly extreme places. I traveled to Thailand multiple times a year for a little over six years. During all those trips, I picked up some of the language, but to be blunt I struggled with it. Thai is tonal, and it can be quite challenging for Americans to pick up on all the subtle complexities of the language's sounds.

We were fortunate, however, to have an amazing team of local translators who went out on the streets and into the brothels and bars with us. The translator I worked with the most, Ying, was very easy to flow and witness with. I would use the bit of Thai that I knew to say hello, and ask a question or two. Usually just enough to get permission to pray with a person and work miracles. God would show up in powerful ways, and the locals would marvel at the reality of His presence and love. But after that I was very limited. I couldn't answer questions. I wasn't able to explain the Gospel in any detail. And I couldn't really lead them in the sinner's prayer. But Ying could. She was brilliant at it.

I have worked with translators worldwide and am grateful for each and every one of them, but Ying was the easiest one to work with. Especially out on the streets. I so appreciated her communication ability to flow not just with me, but so many of our different students. On every trip, we would have dozens of native and non-native English speakers from many different countries. All of whom had different accents, different idioms, and different paces of speech. Ying understood and flowed with all of them.

One day I asked her how she became so fluent with the English language. She told us that for years she'd seen Christians coming to Pattaya, and to her church, who were from the USA, England, Australia, and many other nations. They all spoke English. She felt called by God to help these missionaries, but she didn't speak English. So she asked the Lord to give her the language. One day she woke up and could speak English fluently.

AND OTHER TIMES IT WILL JUST HAPPEN

Early on in my itinerant ministry days I did a lot of house revival meetings. A host would invite us in to minister in their home and we would often see 30, 40, or more people show up. We'd all be packed into the living room, basement, or back patio. We would worship together, dig into the Word, and then I'd pray, prophesy, and minister to people for hours at a time.

One meeting, near Farmington, New Mexico, the Spirit of the Lord fell powerfully during worship. I began singing in tongues. I remember noticing how different it sounded from the tongues I often prayed in, but I knew that tongues could be different at different times for a variety of reasons. So I simply kept singing.

Hours later after the meeting, we were having a time of fellowship. I was leaning against the kitchen counter drinking a cup of tea when a woman walked up to me and commented how much she had appreciated hearing me sing in the native language of her people during worship. She asked me where a "white guy" like me had learned to speak Cree. I told her I wasn't sure what she meant, and said I had simply been singing in tongues while we were worshipping. She told me that whether I knew it or not, I had been singing a native song her Cree grandmother used to sing over her when she was a little girl. She hadn't heard this song in decades, and it had ministered deeply to her.

Through the gift of tongues, God can supernaturally empower us to speak languages we did not previously know. It can happen any time, in a variety of ways. We can ask for it, like Ying did. We can do it without even knowing it, like when I sang in Cree. But we can't initiate this aspect of speaking in tongues. Only God can.

When it comes to praying in tongues, however, we can do that any time we want. So let's look at the power and purpose of praying in tongues.

DECLARING DIVINE MYSTERIES

A little more than 2,000 years ago, at Pentecost, the Holy Spirit was first poured out on believers who were earnestly seeking everything their heavenly Father had for them. The very first manifestation of divine power that they moved in was the gift of tongues (see Acts 2:4). That is quite a ringing endorsement of this gift. Yet there still seems to be a fair amount of confusion and controversy surrounding tongues. Perhaps the simplest and most effective way to set all of that aside, is to point out that it's no wonder the enemy would try to disqualify one of the foundational power tools God has given us. Especially one that is so very effective at equipping, edifying, and empowering the church to be great and mighty witnesses of Jesus.

When we pray in tongues, we are simply accessing the heavenly language we received through the in-filling of the Holy Spirit. This empowers us to proclaim and declare divine mysteries (see 1 Corinthians 14:2). There are several powerful purposes to these supernatural utterances. One of the most important is that praying in tongues strengthens and accelerates us in the things of the Spirit. Another is that praying in tongues allows us to decree, declare, and receive the things of God that are beyond our natural understanding.

BUILD YOURSELF UP IN YOUR MOST HOLY FAITH

As we have already seen, the apostle Paul was a huge fan of praying in tongues. I believe this was because among all of Paul's spiritual gifts and assignments, one of the things he was most passionate about was discipling the churches and believers he was in relationship with. Disciplers love to see those they are working with grow in the things of God, and walk in all they are called to (see 1 Corinthians 14:1). The apostle Paul knew that praying in tongues was so powerful it was almost like a short-cut in the Spirit. That's why he said:

The one who speaks in tongues advances his own spiritual progress... (1 Corinthians 14:4 TPT).

Paul had seen the impact of this in his own life. Remember, Paul had not been saved all that long when he was launched out into an apostolic and evangelical miracle ministry. He traveled from place to place preaching the Gospel, moving in the power of God, and planting churches in multiple regions of the world. On top of all that, this "late-comer" to Jesus partnered with the Holy Spirit to write roughly two-thirds of the New Testament. No wonder he gave thanks to God that he prayed in tongues more than any other (see 1 Corinthians 14:18).

Paul was not boasting when he made that statement. He was revealing a Kingdom secret.

After all, this was the man who referred to himself as the "least" of all the apostles (see 1 Corinthians 15:9). He knew what the power of tongues had done to quickly accelerate, increase, and multiply him in the things of the Kingdom, the strength of his faith, and the fulfillment of His calling. He also knew that it would do the same for absolutely any believer who grabbed hold of the power of tongues.

The apostle Jude agreed. At a critical time in the New Testament church when all sorts of things were trying to divide, dissuade, and disturb believers, Jude wrote his short but very insightful letter to the church. One of the key strategies he gave believers to help them see difficult days become a launchpad into all they were called to, was to pray in the power of the Holy Spirit—in other words, use the heavenly language we receive through His in-filling to pray in tongues. This builds us up in our most holy faith (see Jude 20).

When we pray in tongues, we are edifying, reinforcing, and accelerating every single good thing God has blessed us with through His Son. Gifts, callings, anointings, mantles, fruit, blessings, assignments, glory, awareness of the spiritual realm—all are multiplied and increased by the power of tongues.

THE POWER TO DECLARE YOUR GLORIOUS FUTURE

In multiple places throughout the book of Matthew we see Jesus mentoring the disciples in the power of prayer. One of the keys He shares with them is, *"if you believe, you will receive whatever you ask for in prayer"* (Matthew 21:22 NLT 1996).

All believers have seen examples of this truth in our lives. The most obvious and powerful being our salvation. Every Christian has had that glorious moment when we believed Jesus was real, and that He gave His life for us at the Cross. We prayed the prayer of salvation in faith, asking Him to be our Lord and Savior, and we received eternal life in Christ.

It works the same for every good thing the Father has for us. Whether it's breakthrough, provision, healing, protection, wisdom, favor, or any of the Lord's other promised blessings. We can simply believe, ask, and receive.

But what about the things the Lord has prepared for us that *"No eye has seen, no ear has heard, and no mind has imagined"*? (See First Corinthians 2:9 NLT.) How can we ask for something that we haven't seen or heard of? How can we put into words, let alone a faith-filled prayer, something we've never thought of or even imagined? By the power of praying in tongues.

Tongues allows us to go above and beyond the limits of our natural mind. It takes us out of our heads and into the Spirit. When we pray in tongues, we are praying prayers that are in perfect agreement with the plans and purposes of God. Even His plans and purposes of which we don't yet have any natural understanding or concept.

THE POWER TO "BIRTH" YOUR GLORIOUS FUTURE

I'd been a believer for about six months when I had a powerful encounter with the Holy Spirit. He took me into an elementary school classroom and started teaching me my new heavenly language. He gave me a few key words to say, and instructed me to repeat them over and over again.

Not long after that encounter, I came across a book by Mahesh Chavda titled *The Hidden Power of Speaking in Tongues*. One of the things Mahesh shared in his book was how praying in tongues was a secret to seeing amazing things of God birthed in a believer's life. As a new Christian, I was hungry for everything that the Lord had for me. So I committed to praying in tongues for at least 30 minutes a day for the next 40 days in a row.

During those six weeks while I was praying in tongues, I never really sensed much of anything going on. That's the thing about tongues. Its power is not in our understanding. Its power is not in what we might see, feel, or experience when we are praying in the spirit. The power of tongues is that it lets us pray deep unto deep, spirit to Spirit, divinely inspired prayers that are in perfect agreement with the plans and purposes of God. When we're praying in tongues, we're decreeing and declaring in the spirit what is well beyond our natural ability to understand. No wonder tongues accelerates the things of God in our life.

It wasn't long after those 40 days of praying in tongues that my life radically changed. The Lord called me into full-time ministry, and He connected me with two of the most important people in my life—my dear friends Ron and Patricia King—who became my spiritual parents and mentors. After a few months of doing inner-city prophetic and miracle evangelism with them in different parts of Canada, they invited me to be part of launching the USA arm of their ministry. I moved from Montana to Phoenix, Arizona, and traveled with them full-time for almost a year. Then I was launched out into what became a global itinerant ministry under their covering. As a new believer, I hadn't heard, seen, or even imagined any of that. But I know it all came forth through those days and hours of praying in tongues.

ACTIVATE THE POWER OF TONGUES

If you have received the baptism of the Holy Spirit, then you have the gift of tongues. You may need to stir it up, but you have it. I've found the gift of tongues works a lot like a muscle. The more you use it, the stronger it gets. And as Christians, we definitely want to use this power tool that God has blessed us with as much as possible.

So let's get you activated in the power of praying in tongues.

1. Just do it.

It's actually that simple. The way to activate the power of tongues is to use the gift of tongues. If you've been praying in tongues for years, keep doing it. If you've never prayed in tongues, all you have to do is start.

2. Commit to a set amount of time.

Remember, the gift of tongues is like a muscle. The more you use it the more powerful it gets. For the next week, commit to praying in tongues every day for a set amount of time. You don't have to start with thirty minutes a day like I did. Any amount of time spent praying in tongues is powerful, and will bear good fruit. Consider starting with just five minutes a day. We waste five minutes on inconsequential things again and again throughout our days. So why not commit to investing five minutes a day to praying in tongues. It's as simple as setting a timer on your phone.

3. Build up your power.

Now that you're praying in tongues every day. Start to build up your strength. After your first week of praying in tongues for five minutes a day, add an additional five minutes. That has you up to ten minutes a day for a week. Consider adding five minutes every week until you're up to thirty minutes a day. If that seems like too much, add one minute a day each week.

4. When you don't know what to pray, pray in tongues.

At times, we all have situations that seem overwhelming. When I don't know what to pray or how to pray, I know it's time to pray in tongues. Whether it's a wayward prodigal, a terminal diagnosis, a difficult relationship, or any other "impossible" problem, hold it in your heart and mind and begin to pray in tongues. Know that as you do, you are partnering with God to birth His perfect plans for breakthrough and turnaround.

– 8 –

Power of Righteousness

For He made Him who
knew no sin to be sin for us,
that we might become the
righteousness of God in Him
(2 Corinthians 5:21 NKJV).

BY the end of this chapter, you are going to realize that the Lord has blessed you with a global ministry. One that reaches the whole wide world each and every day. I'm not talking about a show on all the Christian networks. Or a top-selling book. And I don't mean livestreaming on the Internet. Those are all great, but this is even bigger. I'm talking about the power of righteousness. Every time you choose to operate in it, you reach all of creation.

When you said yes to Jesus, you were sanctified, set apart, and made holy by the blood of the Lamb. You are now the very righteousness of God in Christ (see 2 Corinthians 5:21). That not only means you've been made right with God through Christ. It means that in Christ you are once again restored to your God-intended, God-ordained, God-created "original settings" of Genesis 1:26-28. You're once again in His image. And once again able to walk with Him, empowered to be His representative throughout the earth.

The way you do all that is by choosing to walk in your born-again nature as opposed to your old carnal nature. When you do, you are walking in the power of righteousness. You are re-presenting Him everywhere you go. And it has much further-reaching impact than most Christians have ever realized or even imagined.

ALL OF CREATION IS WAITING

While most believers have yet to fully grasp how truly glorious the power of righteousness is, creation is well aware of it. And it can't wait for us to wake up and realize it according to Romans 8:19 (NKJV): "...creation eagerly waits for the revealing of the sons of God."

While the word *righteousness* never appears in Romans 8:19, the concept is very much there. In Greek, there are several different words that can be used for *son*, and there are important distinctions between them that have to do with stages of development. The word for *sons* used in Romans 8:19 is *huios*. This Greek word very specifically refers to "mature" sons—ones who have grown to resemble their father in character and nature, and are now recognized publicly as his representatives.

I want to be clear that the use of the word *sons* in Romans 8:19 in no way leaves out women. Remember, there is no male or female in Christ Jesus (see Galatians 3:28). That doesn't mean that there aren't two different genders. It means that anything available to men in Christ is also available to women. Creation is waiting eagerly for mature female believers to realize who they are just as much as it's waiting eagerly for mature male believers.

The key idea in Romans 8:19 is that it is *huios* who are needed. *Mature* believers.

Hebrews 5:14 tells us what it is to be mature in the things of God. My favorite version of that Scripture is in the 1996 New Living Translation where it points out that mature ones *"recognize the difference between right and wrong, and then do what is right."* Notice that mature ones do not decide according to their carnal nature or soulish desires what is right or wrong, but recognize according to the will and ways of God what is good and what is evil. And then mature ones *choose* to do what is right. In other words, they choose to walk in righteousness.

This is what all of creation is eagerly waiting for.

This is what all of creation is keenly anticipating.

The whole wide world and everything in it longs for believers like you to wake up to who you truly are in Christ, and choose to walk in the power of righteousness. Because when you do—when you walk according to God's will and ways instead of according to your old carnal nature—you represent your heavenly Father here on earth. You are actually re-presenting Him. That ripples throughout all of creation. There's clear evidence of this in Romans 5:18-19 (NLT):

> *Yes, Adam's one sin brings condemnation for everyone, but Christ's one act of righteousness brings a right relationship with God and new life for everyone. Because one person disobeyed God, many became sinners. But because one other person obeyed God, many will be made righteous.*

When Adam chose to not walk according to God's will and ways, it didn't only affect him. It actually impacted everyone, everywhere, for all time. When a child of God refuses to walk in righteousness, we need to catch that it not only brings darkness into his or her life, it also releases darkness throughout the world.

The good news, however, is what Romans 5:18-19 shows us about Christ. It says that when He chose to obey, it was not Him who was made righteous—He already was—but righteousness was released on earth. His act of obedience blessed all people in all places for all time.

Adam was a son. Jesus is *the* Son. The choices that sons and daughters of God make, impact and affect the whole wide world.

YOUR CHOICES MAKE A DIFFERENCE

In Christ, you have been made right with God. You have been restored to the fullness of relationship with your heavenly Father. You are a child of God (see Romans 8:15 and Galatians 3:26). That means you are powerful. Every time you choose to walk in righteousness, you are making a real difference in the world.

Your decisions not only affect your life, but they affect all of creation. That is not a burdensome responsibility; it is a truly glorious opportunity.

Sin has repercussions. Most believers understand that. We know unrighteousness has a negative effect in our lives. We need to also understand that when we choose to sin there are implications that ripple through all of creation. But here's the good news. Righteousness is way more powerful than sin. Jesus is our proof of that. His choosing to walk in righteousness here on earth absolved us of all sin, defeated the enemy, and overcame death. While we are, obviously, not the Christ, we are in Him and also have His Spirit of holiness and righteousness living inside us. In Christ, and by the power of His Holy Spirit, we can choose to walk in the imputed righteousness of our born-again nature, as opposed to following the urges and bents of our old carnal ways. When we do choose righteousness, it is released out into the world.

Good is more powerful than evil (see Romans 12:21). Light is more powerful than darkness (see Genesis 1:3). And choosing to walk in righteousness has a powerful impact on the world and everything in it. I realize it doesn't always look and feel like this is true, but it is. The Bible says so. And Jesus proved it.

Choose to walk in sin and darkness, and you release sin and darkness into the world. But, and this is huge, choose to walk in righteousness, and righteousness breaks forth. Choose to walk in the character and nature of your heavenly Father, and you are representing (or quite literally re-presenting) Him to all creation. Choose to walk in love, patience, faithfulness, joy, mercy, kindness, or forgiveness at any given moment, and they are released throughout the earth. That's the power of righteousness.

When we catch this it changes everything. It's no longer a burden to resist the enemy. It's no longer a chore to say no to temptation. It's an opportunity. When we choose not to give into our old carnality, but instead choose to operate from our born-again nature, we are walking as enlightened and empowered children of God, gloriously influencing all of creation. That's the power of righteousness.

THE SOLUTION FOR DARK DAYS

We find ourselves in the midst of some dark days. Wickedness is everywhere. Sin abounds. Corruption runs rampant. Governments, school systems, media, and more have given place to depravity, lies, manipulation, and even flat-out evil. But none of this has taken God by surprise, and He is not undone or discouraged by it. He has a plan. It will work. And it involves His people understanding and choosing to walk in the power of righteousness. He outlines this in Isaiah 60:2-3 (NASB):

> *For behold, darkness will cover the earth and deep darkness the peoples; but the Lord will rise upon you and His glory will appear upon you. Nations will come to your light, and kings to the brightness of your rising.*

Let's examine those verses a bit. *"Darkness will cover the earth and deep darkness the peoples."* Sound familiar? If you've been paying attention to world events, or checked in with the news even occasionally, you see that these are the times in which we are living. Darkness throughout the earth. And deep darkness on people everywhere. But God's response to all of this is not to tell us to duck and cover. Or to be afraid or frustrated. Or to be critical and bitter about it all. No. He outlines clearly what the answer is—His people allowing the Lord to *"rise upon"* them, and letting His glory *"appear upon"* them. In other words, those who choose to re-present Him. His presence and power, absolutely, but also His character and nature. His glorious fullness. His likeness. His righteousness.

Too often we think things like, *Well if God really wanted to do something about this mess, He could just snap His fingers and take care of it.* And sure, He could. He's sovereign. Always has been, and always will be. But like we talked about in a previous chapter, His sovereign plan since Day Six has been to have a people who are willing to walk with Him as His dominion stewards on earth. His plan is you walking in the power of righteousness, which ripples throughout all of creation. Or as Isaiah 60:3 (NASB) puts it, *"Nations will come to your light, and kings to the brightness of your rising."*

The issues of our day aren't nearly so much about there being too much darkness in the world. They're because there's not enough light. You can change that. Light shatters darkness. Choose to walk in the power of righteousness, and you release His light throughout all creation.

BE DIFFERENT

When we choose righteousness, we're walking in who we truly are in Christ. That means we're going to look different, sound different, and be different from the rest of the world. This is powerful. Isaiah 60:3 points out that many will be drawn to us specifically because they see or sense something different about us. Sure, we've all had people reject us when we tried to tell them about Jesus. But when we walk in who we truly are in Christ, that radical righteousness and heroic holiness actually draws interest because it is so different.

People everywhere see the systems of the world failing them in so many ways right now. They're hungry for something different. They're hungry for something they can believe in, and count on. They're hungry for something greater than themselves. When we walk in righteousness, we're re-presenting the One they're truly hungry for, even if they don't yet realize it.

I told you about the trips I led for years to Pattaya, Thailand. We would regularly see revivals break out on the streets and in the brothel bars. A big part of what opened the door for that was our choosing to walk in righteousness while we were there. Everywhere we went, people noticed we were different, and they were drawn to us because of it.

On the surface, I didn't really look all that different from the majority of the men visiting Pattaya. I was a white dude in his forties. Most of the sex tourists in Pattaya were male, white, and in the second half of life. When I walked into a brothel bar with our teams, the girls would come up to me to ply their trade. Very quickly, however, they discovered that I was different. That's when things always got interesting.

After they offered themselves to me—not always that directly, but always very obviously—I would respond, "Oh, that's not what I'm here for." They were always taken aback by that statement. Amazed. I could practically hear them thinking, *But that's what everybody's here for?! If you're not here for that, what the heck are you doing here?!* And then I would share with them that I was there because my God, Jesus Christ, loved them so much that He brought me all the way from Phoenix, Arizona, in the United Stated of America so I could pray with them. I can't think of a single time when one of the women didn't let us pray. Most had radical encounters with the reality of God, and many got saved.

What opened the door for all of that? Being different from the world. That's the power of righteousness.

ACTIVATE THE POWER OF RIGHTEOUSNESS

Romans 14:17 points out that the very first aspect of the Kingdom of God is righteousness. So when we choose to walk in righteousness, we are cooperating with God to see His Kingdom come and His will be done here on earth. That's how powerful righteousness is. That's why when we choose it, it ripples through all of creation. Righteousness helps establish His Kingdom here on earth.

So let's get you activated in the power of righteousness.

1. Realize the choices you make have impact.

The world tells us that if we don't have big names, big platforms, or big bank accounts, then we don't really matter. Nothing could be further from the truth. You are a child of God. You are the bride of Christ. You are the very righteousness of God and are filled with His Holy Spirit. When you choose to walk in that—when you choose to walk in love, peace, joy, patience, kindness, hope, faith, or mercy—you are releasing His light out into this dark world. You are shifting atmospheres, affecting lives, and impacting creation.

2. Recognize that temptation is not failure, it's opportunity.

The enemy likes to try to convince us that if we're wrestling with temptation, we've already failed. But we need to understand that temptation is not sin. Jesus was tempted in all things, and yet He never sinned (see Hebrews 4:15). Temptation is actually opportunity. When you're tempted, it's your chance to choose righteousness. When you do, you're not just "hanging in there" and resisting the enemy, you are walking in authority and power and righteousness. You are making a difference, and are part of God's solution.

3. Understand righteousness isn't legalism.

Choosing to operate in righteousness has nothing to do with legalism or having a works mentality. There is nothing "religious" or "sanctimonious" about it. We don't choose to walk in righteousness to prove how holy we are. Or to earn God's love and approval. Or to get Him to bless us. God already loves us. He has already done all, won all, and given all. There is nothing He is withholding, so there is nothing righteousness "gets" us. We choose to walk in righteousness because we realize it's who we truly are in Christ, and because we understand that there is real power in it.

4. Spend time in the Word so you know who you truly are.

There's no better way to know who you truly are in Christ than to read your Bible. It will remind you of all that you've been given, all that you have, and all that you can walk in. Read the Bible knowing that you were made in God's image. Read the Bible knowing that you are meant to be an expression of His character and nature, His goodness, and His righteousness. And then choose to walk in it all. The Bible will help you remember who you truly are, and with that revelation of identity comes the realization of opportunity.

5. We don't do the "right" thing to get a right result.

There are times you will choose to walk in righteousness, and not see any kind of immediate "result." That's okay. We don't do the right thing to get a certain result, we do it to honor and cooperate with the Righteous One who dwells within us. We do it because we know when we choose righteousness it has power that ripples throughout the earth. Don't base your choice to walk in righteousness on an expected result, base it on knowing it is who you are in Christ.

6. Look different, sound different, be different.

When you walk in righteousness you will look different, sound different, and act different from those around you. Be loving. Be compassionate. Have integrity. Be happy. Keep your word. Be trustworthy. Be filled with faith, hope, and positive expectation when the rest of the world thinks everything is dark, dire, and doomed. Your family will notice. Your coworkers will notice. The people of your community will notice. And they will be drawn to it.

– 9 –

Power of Decree

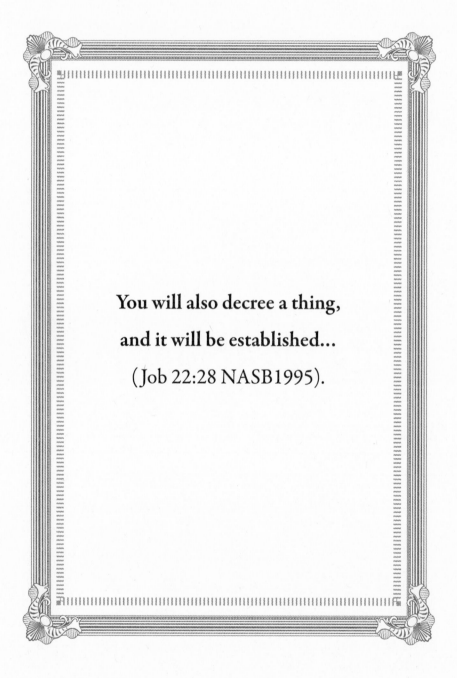

You will also decree a thing,

and it will be established...

(Job 22:28 NASB1995).

THE very first realm of Kingdom power that God puts on display in the Bible is the power of decree. It is right there at the very beginning in Genesis 1:1-3. He speaks. The Word goes forth. And everything changes. God decrees, *"Let there be light,"* and BOOM! There is light. God then continues on for the next 22 verses to speak forth all of creation.

Genesis 1:1-25 clearly shows us the power of decree. The Word of God is declared, and it has radical impact here on earth.

Immediately after that, in Genesis 1:26, God makes us in His image and after His likeness. When you look at the original Hebrew, it's very clear that He is not being repetitive when He says that we are made in His image and after His likeness. Being made in His image (the Hebrew word *tselem*) means we are to be His representatives here on earth. Being made after His likeness (the Hebrew word *demuth*) means we resemble Him and share a similar manner. The former has to do with what we are here to do. The latter helps reveal how we do it. We are created in His image and after His likeness, to operate in His authority, by the power of His Spirit, to tend to His creation. One of the ways we do this is the very way our Father brought creation forth. Through the power of decree.

The power of decree, and our ability to move in it, is reinforced throughout Scripture. Probably the clearest declaration of the certain power of decree is in Isaiah 55:11 where the Lord promises that when His Word goes forth it never returns void, accomplishes all it is sent to do, and always bears fruit. In other words, when we decree the Word of the Lord we can be certain it will have impact.

And just in case you're wondering if only the Lord can decree His Word, or if you also can move in this mighty Kingdom power, Jeremiah 1:9-10 (NLT) settles that:

...Look, I have put my words in your mouth! Today I appoint you to stand up against nations and kingdoms. Some you must uproot and tear down, destroy and overthrow. Others you must build up and plant.

God is pointing out to Jeremiah that He has put His words in Jeremiah's mouth as power tools that will help him deal with what is going on in the nations and kingdoms of the earth. When Jeremiah decrees the Word of the Lord, it will work against the things of darkness—uprooting them, tearing them down, destroying, and overthrowing them. It will also work to plant and build up the things of Heaven here on earth. That's the power of decree.

This passage of Scripture comes right after Jeremiah tries to find reasons why he couldn't possibly be qualified to flow in the power of decree and speak the Word of the Lord (see Jeremiah 1:6). The Lord immediately affirms Jeremiah in the power of decree, letting him know that all he needs to do is follow God's lead and declare His Word (see Jeremiah 1:7). This affirmation is not just for great prophets like Jeremiah. It's for every believer. It's for you. After all, remember what Jesus Himself said about you in Matthew 11:11. Even if you are the least in the Kingdom of Heaven, you are still greater than even the greatest of the Old Testament prophets. You are made and meant to flow in the power of decree.

Let's look at one more Scripture about the power of decree. It's one of my favorites, and it's the one that started this chapter.

You will also decree a thing, and it will be established for you; and light will shine on your ways (Job 22:28 NASB1995).

That most certainly settles it. If you had any doubt of whether or not anyone other than God Himself, or just His big-name prophets, could flow in the power of decree, Job 22:28 makes it clear it is for every believer—including you. *You* (yes, you). *Will also decree a thing* (not just God and His recognized prophets, but you *will also*). *And it will be established for you* (let's repeat that one last time to make sure you really get it...*for you*). And just in case even all of that isn't clear enough, it is capped off with an allusion harkening back to Genesis 1:3 promising that when you make decrees it releases light to shine.

The power of decree shatters darkness.

The power of decree tears down the works of the enemy.

The power of decree establishes the reality of God's will and ways on earth.

The power of decree sends forth the Word of the Lord, putting it to work in your life and your spheres of influence. It will not return void. It will bear fruit. And it will accomplish what it is sent to do.

I have seen the power of decree work time and time again.

THE POWER OF DECREE CAN OPEN NATIONS!

Several years ago, I was frequently serving in Eastern Europe. I would often take several trips a year to minister throughout the Baltic region and in the nation of Latvia. Plus there was a very respected immunologist, and some outstanding labs and medical facilities where I could get affordable, cutting-edge care for the health challenges I was overcoming back then. As a U.S. citizen I was only allowed to be in the Eurozone for three months at a time, and for no more than a total of six months each year. I would usually max out my annual tourist visa by August or

September. Some friends, who were leaders in Latvia's government, had the excellent idea of helping me get set up to apply for legal residency in their nation. That way I could spend as much time as I needed in Latvia, the Baltic nations, and all of the Eurozone.

The day I was scheduled to meet with the immigration official assigned to my application, I showed up with a file folder filled with all the required forms, documentation, legal, and financial information. We spent over an hour going through all my paperwork. Everything was in order. But then right at the end, when it came time to pay the fees involved, we ran into some administrative minutiae. The official told me that I was not allowed to pay cash and that I had to use a bank card to prove I had an active account. Not a problem. I pulled out my credit card and handed it to him. He scowled at it, and began to shake his head no. I asked him what the issue was. He told me that because the name on the credit card I was paying with was not the same as the name on my legal identification (my U.S. passport), my application could not be processed.

"Wait a minute," I said, "what do you mean there are different names on the documents? They both clearly say *Robert Hotchkin*."

His head wagged no again, and he repeated his assertion. "They are different. Your passport shows your name as *Robert B Hotchkin*, but the credit card says *Robert Hotchkin*. They are not the same."

I pointed out that it was obviously the same name. "Look at the picture on my passport," I told him. "You can clearly see that it's me." I explained that "B" was simply my middle initial and my passport listed it, but my credit card did not.

This time he simply said, "No. They are not the same."

I turned to a friend who had come with me to translate if need be. I was thinking there must be a language issue. She could tell I was getting frustrated, and encouraged me to take a deep breath. She explained it was not a language issue so much as a bureaucracy issue, and that this was simply how the process tended to work there. I slumped back in the chair, not sure what to do, obviously exasperated. The administrator looked at me, smiled, and confirmed that it indeed was not a problem of language, "I understand what you are saying, but I do not have the authority to do anything about it. This will not be approved at the next level so there is no need to continue."

When he told me he did not have the authority to do anything in this situation a lightbulb went off for me. He might not have the authority, but I knew who did. Me. In Christ. Armed with the power of decree.

I asked if I could be excused for a few minutes. He said yes, certainly, but it would put me back in the queue. He let me know that nothing would be different with another appointment, but handed me a slip of paper with a number on it and told me I would be called when it was my turn again.

I went back to the waiting area and found a place where I could stand and pray. There were some waist-high shelves along one wall where I placed my Bible. I opened up to Exodus 23:20-23 and 33:1-2. In both passages God promises to overcome enemies and obstacles to bring His people into the land He has prepared for us. I began to praise Him, and decree His Word:

> *Lord, thank You that You are not undone by anything happening here today. In the name of Your Son Jesus, I decree that You are sending forth angels from Heaven to safely and easily lead me into this land that You have prepared for me so I may live here according to Your plans and purposes. Praise You that Your angels*

provide instructions and strategies, while clearing the
way of all resistance. In Jesus's mighty name, I decree
that every obstacle is removed, and every enemy is
driven from my midst!

I might not have been dealing with Canaanites, Amorites, Hittites, Perizzites, Hivites, and Jebusites, but there were certainly bureaucracy-ites, administration-ites, red-tape-ites, and minutiae-ites that were standing in the way. I did not raise my voice or make any kind of a ruckus or scene. I simply inhabited my authority in Christ, knowing the power of decree, and sent forth His Word.

I continued to pray in faith, under my breath, until I could sense a shift. Then I found a seat, and waited for my number to be called. As I waited, I received wisdom and strategy. The problem was that my passport listed my middle initial, but my form of payment did not. So all I needed was a new form of payment.

About an hour later my number was called. I ended up back at the same administrator's desk. I asked if this could all be resolved with a bank card that included my middle initial. He said, "Yes, of course, if the name matches there is no problem."

The next morning I made arrangements back home to have a debit card that included my middle initial express-mailed to me. In less than a week it was in my hand, and I was back at the immigration official's desk. My legal resident status was approved. All thanks to administrative breakthroughs, angelic assistance, and divine solutions that were put into motion by the power of decree.

THE POWER OF DECREE CAN SHAPE YOUR FUTURE

The power of decree not only can be used to impact your current circumstances, it can also be wielded to shape your future.

Years ago, when my wife and I were going through premarital counseling, we received some excellent advice from our dear friend and spiritual mother, Patricia King. She suggested that we seek the Lord for Scriptures we could declare over our marriage to "frame and establish" it in the spirit even before we stepped into it in the natural. I thought the idea was brilliant. After all, many engaged couples build a house to move into together after they're married. The home is framed and established, waiting to cover, keep, and protect them when they start their new life together as husband and wife. If this can be done in the natural with wood and nails, how much more can it be done in the spirit with Scripture and decrees? After all, the Word of God is more solid and unwavering than any building materials of man.

So we took time to seek the Lord and ask Him to highlight Scriptures we could use as decrees to form and inform our future life together. As ever, He was faithful. For the next few weeks the Lord kept highlighting Scriptures and pointing out promises. By the time He was done, we had pages of decrees that covered every area of a man and woman bringing their lives together in holy matrimony.

During the weeks and months leading up to our wedding, we prayed these decrees every day. We also asked our intercessors if they would join us in making the decrees.

It was powerful. We were surprised by blessing upon blessing as we approached our wedding day. And maybe most miraculous of all, none of the stress of planning a major life event seemed to touch us. We had a great grace to enjoy one another and our families throughout it all.

Many people told us that the first year of marriage was the most challenging, especially when marrying later in life like we did. But our first year actually felt like it was "bathed in butter." The decrees worked. And they continue to work. I know, because we still use them. Like any busy couple, we occasionally have stresses and disagreements. And, yes, we have had a few bumps along the way in our many years of marriage and with our extended families. But I marvel at the power of the decrees the Lord gave us back when we were engaged. Whenever we hit one of those "bumps," the Lord would nudge me to get those decrees back out and pray through them. It would always shift atmospheres, reveal solutions, and reinforce the firm foundation of Kingdom values our marriage is built upon. The Word of God never fails.

ACTIVATE THE POWER OF DECREE

One of the reasons there is so much power in making Scripture-based decrees is because when we make a decree we are sending forth the Word. John 1:14 tells us that Jesus is the Word made flesh. So when we send forth the Word of God in a decree, it is like injecting the truth, power, and reality of Jesus into the situation. When we send forth the Word, we are sending forth the power of the One who saves, the One who heals, the One who delivers, the One who restores, the One who revives, the One for whom nothing is impossible.

Following are keys to help you unlock the power of decree.

1. Find a promise of God to stand on.

Whatever situation you're facing or circumstance you're dealing with, there is a promise in God's Word for you to stand on. For example, does it seem like your prodigal is getting farther and farther away from the Lord? Well, Acts 16:31 promises that if you call upon the name of the Lord you will be saved and *all* of your household. That includes your prodigal. Just like Romans 10:20 and Isaiah 65:1 promise that He *will* reveal Himself to those who are not seeking Him, and show Himself to those who are not looking for Him. Your prodigal may not be going after God, but God is going after your prodigal.

2. Meditate on the promise.

Focus on the truth of God's Word. Let it become more real and more true to you than the situation you're facing. You are not denying the facts in front of you, you are allowing the certain truth of God's Word to be more real to you than the current facts you are facing. Facts change. Truth does not.

3. Turn the promise into a decree.

Take the promise and craft it into a decree. For example, we can take the Scriptures from Acts and Romans and turn them into the following decree:

> *I declare that I have called upon the name of my Lord, Jesus Christ. Because of that, I am saved, and all of my household. Lord, I decree that includes my prodigal. I decree that she is saved. I decree that it is settled in the*

spirit, and You are bringing it about in the natural. Thank You, Lord, that You are revealing Yourself to my prodigal. That You are showing Yourself to her. I decree that You are making Yourself real to my prodigal. I decree that You are shining Your light into the darkness that is trying to draw her away from You. In Jesus's name I decree it!

4. Decree the Word in faith until...

Send forth the Word, knowing it is working and bearing fruit. Do not give up. Do not give in. Do not stop decreeing until you see it fully made so. The Word you are decreeing will not return void. Think of Moses in the book of Exodus. He had the Word of the Lord: *"Let my people go."* He had to decree it again and again and again. Eventually it fully came to pass. And so will the Word that you are decreeing!

– 10 –

Power of Favor

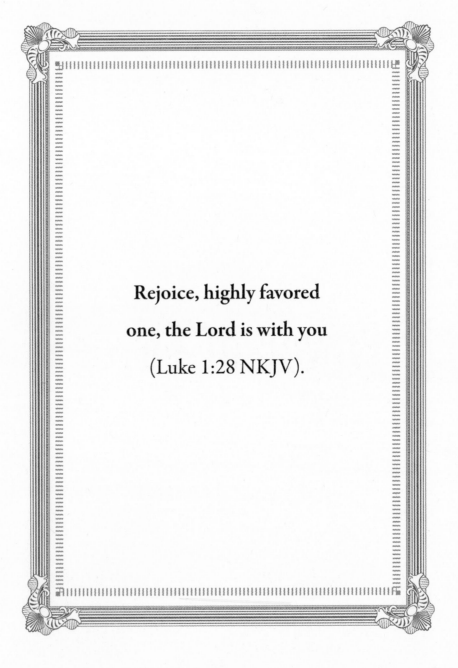

Rejoice, highly favored
one, the Lord is with you
(Luke 1:28 NKJV).

THERE are few things as powerful as favor. When you walk in the favor of the Lord, it is like having your feet bathed in butter. The right doors open. The right connections happen. Promotions come. Opportunities present themselves. You're noticed. You're preferred. You're thought well of.

The power of favor is like being magnetized to attract blessings. Good things just seem to happen. You can't really explain it, and you don't need to. It's simply the power of favor.

According to Luke 2:52, Jesus walked in favor during His time here on earth. A favor that increased and grew. Remember that Jesus is our Messiah, and our Model. As our Messiah, He came to restore us to relationship with our heavenly Father and His Kingdom here on earth. As our Model, He also came to show us what it looks like to walk in that restored relationship (see John 14:12). Does that mean miracles, signs, and wonders? Absolutely. But it also means walking in favor with God, and with man, that increases over time. Jesus told us that as the Father sent Him, so He also sends us (see John 20:21). That means because Jesus was sent in divine favor to help Him achieve His Father's purposes here on earth, so are you.

The New Testament Greek word for *favor* is *charis*. It can be translated many ways, including: "divine influence," "benefit," "gift," and "grace." It comes from a root word that means to be "well off" and to "do well." The power of favor means that you can be confident that God is with you, He is for you, and He is working on your behalf to assure that you walk in and achieve all that you were created for and called to.

FAVOR OPENS DOORS AND MAKES THINGS HAPPEN

Several years ago, when I was still fairly new in ministry, I was invited to be part of a prophetic roundtable discussion. A well-known publisher was hosting the evening. They wanted to hear from different prophetic voices what the Lord was saying about the season we were entering. We each took a few minutes to share what we had been hearing from the Lord, and briefly outlined key messages He had given us for the coming year. The fact that I had even been invited to participate was a sign of favor. But it didn't end there.

Part of the evening included a catered dinner. Despite there being many, much-better-known ministers in attendance, when we sat down to eat, the senior editor of the publishing house chose to sit at my table. The editor also spent most of the dinner talking with me. By the time we were done eating, she asked if I would be interested in publishing with them. There were several topics I had touched on in our conversation that she thought would make for excellent books. I was asked to submit a proposal.

A couple of weeks later, when a friend of mine found out I was about to sign a book deal with this well-known publisher, she mentioned someone she knew who had thought about submitting ideas to this same publishing house years before, but had been told he needed a literary agent to even be considered.

I didn't have an agent. I wasn't a well-known speaker back then. I didn't have a name most people would recognize or respond to. And I hadn't done much TV or other media at that point. There was no reason for me to be preferred over all those other better-known and more experienced speakers, ministers, and authors.

I simply had favor.

And you have it too.

YOU ARE HIGHLY FAVORED

When you have favor, you are held in high regard. You're given special treatment and showered with blessings that you haven't earned and don't really deserve. Favor makes you the beneficiary of all sorts of goodwill.

Imagine what an advantage you would have if you were a member of a wealthy, influential family. Or if you were very close friends with the president of the United States, the queen of England, the CEO of a top tech firm, or some major celebrity who used their name, position, and authority to open doors and make connections for you. Everywhere you went, people would be pointing you out. They would want to be seen with you, and talk to you. That would be favor in the natural.

You have something much greater than that in the spirit.

Forget world leaders, royalty, famous people, or media and business moguls. You have the wisest, most powerful, most loving and benevolent Being of all time and space on your side and working on your behalf. The King of kings, the Lord of lords, God Almighty, your heavenly Father calls you His friend, His child, and His heir (see John 15:15 and Romans 8:16-17). He walks with you, will never leave you nor forsake you, and He goes before you to light your path and make your way (see Deuteronomy 31:8; Hebrews 13:5; Psalm 119:105). Now that's favor!

FAVOR GROWS AND INCREASES

This is how much favor you have. Before you ever even knew the Lord, He laid down His life for you.

Think about that.

Even when you were still given over to darkness and in love with the world's wicked ways, you had so much favor with God that He chose to go to the Cross and pay the debt for your sins so that you could be restored to relationship with Him. He did for you what you could not possibly do for yourself. He wanted you, way before you wanted Him. You had done nothing for Him, yet He gave everything for you. That's some powerful favor.

Yes, God was on your side before you even knew Him. But it doesn't end there. You are actually growing in divine favor. Now that you belong to Him, God declares that He has given you everything (see Ephesians 1:3; 2 Peter 1:3)—including complete, utter, and total access to Him. Members of the president's Cabinet don't have total access to POTUS. The prime minister of England can't simply step into the presence of the queen anytime he wants. Yet as a believer, you now have that kind of favor with God. Hebrews 4:16 (NKJV) says so:

> *Let us therefore come boldly to the throne of grace, that we may obtain mercy and find grace to help in time of need.*

That *"in time of need"* phrase shows you the level of favor you have. It's not just on your good days when you have been a "super" Christian leading the lost to the Lord, working miracles, reading your Bible for hours a day, and praying in tongues and decreeing Scripture. It's not just when you can point to something and say, "Hey Lord, I earned my way into a meeting with You." No. God declares in His Word that you are so favored that you can come to Him any time you want, with whatever you need, even when you have made a mess of things. You are highly favored.

YOU ALSO HAVE FAVOR WITH OTHERS

The powerful favor you walk in is not only with God, but also with people.

Psalm 5:12 promises that God surrounds you with divine favor as a shield. That means in addition to favor magnetizing you for blessings, opening doors, and creating opportunities, it also defends you against enemies. Just like in Genesis 26:28. When King Abimelech saw that Isaac walked in the favor of the Lord, he no longer wanted to oppose him. He wanted to be allies with Isaac. He even gave him an advantageous piece of property as part of the treaty he drew up. The favor of God can turn your most aggressive enemy into one of your most ardent supporters.

That word *surrounds* in Psalm 5:12 is the Hebrew word *atar,* and it can also be translated as "to crown." That's what favor does. It "crowns" you. It marks you as someone special in the spirit. People are drawn to you. They want to work with you. They want to be connected with you. They open doors for you. They share their resources with you.

That's the power or favor.

ACTIVATE THE POWER OF FAVOR

You are blessed and highly favored. It is important that you see and understand that. If you have not yet fully experienced the power of favor, that doesn't mean you do not have it. It simply means you haven't activated it yet. It's like thinking you don't have a car in the garage, because you haven't driven it lately. It's there. You just need to grab the keys and go start it up. So let's look at how you can activate the realm of favor that you've been blessed with.

1. Reject rejection.

Don't look to the past and try to come up with examples of why you don't feel favored. Let go of the times you were not received, or when things didn't work out. Even if it was only a month ago. Or yesterday. That is not your portion. You're not made for rejection. You're not made to be left out or left behind. You are blessed and highly favored.

2. Realize that not every "no" is a lack of favor.

Yes, when you are favored good things happen, and doors tend to open. But it's important to realize that a "no" is not evidence of a lack of favor. Sometimes God is protecting us from something. Or saving us for something better. When a door closes or an opportunity does not come to pass, remember that you are blessed and highly favored. Know that God is there, and that He is leading you into His very best for you. The right doors will open at the right time.

3. Ask God to activate the power of favor in your life.

In John 14:14, Jesus lets us know that we can ask for anything that the Father has promised us, and we will receive it. You saw all through this chapter that you have been promised divine and increasing favor. Ask, in the name of Jesus, for the Lord to activate that favor at all new levels in your life.

4. Decree that you have favor.

Job 22:28 says that if you decree a thing it shall be established. Perhaps the single most powerful way to activate the power of favor in your life is to declare in faith that you have it. Take Scriptures about favor, and decree them over yourself every morning before you leave home, and every night before you go to bed. Frame your life with the power of favor (re-read Chapter 9 for a reminder of how powerful scriptural decrees are). Here is an example:

> *I am blessed and highly favored. I am crowned with favor. I am surrounded with favor. Everywhere I go, I walk in the favor and blessings of God. The right doors open for me. Kingdom connections happen for me. Blessings are drawn to me. Every day I grow in favor with God and man. My life is marked by ever-increasing and ever-multiplying favor* (from Luke 1:28; Luke 2:52; Deuteronomy 28:6; Psalm 23:5-6; Isaiah 22:22).

5. Sow favor.

The law of sowing and reaping works in all things, including favor. To grow in favor, sow some favor. Ask the Lord to highlight someone to whom you can show favor. When He does, show them favor. Compliment them. Encourage them. Sow into their ministry or calling. Be a blessing. Show them the type of favor you expect in your own life. And then, after you have sown favor, call in your harvest of favor. The more generously you sow favor, the more abundantly you will reap (activate) favor in your life (see 2 Corinthians 9:6).

– 11 –

Power of
Giving Thanks

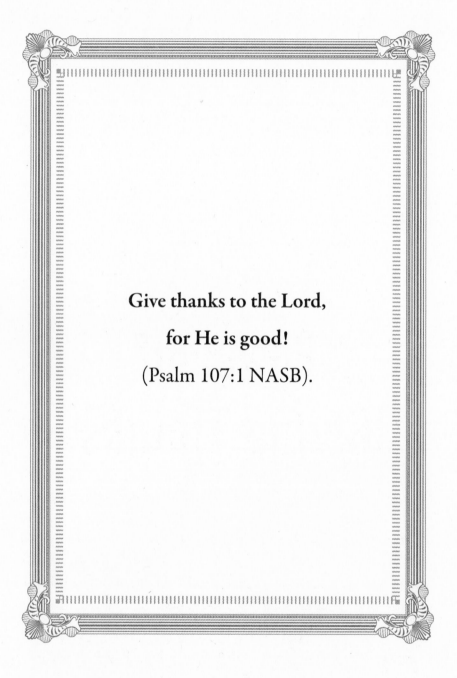

Give thanks to the Lord,

for He is good!

(Psalm 107:1 NASB).

WHEN we say, "Thank you," it's usually in response to a gift, a kind act, or a service someone has done for us. We think of it as being polite. But it's actually much more than that. Giving thanks is a realm of power in the Kingdom of God. A realm that taps us into miracles of increase and multiplication.

In Matthew 15:32-38 we see a situation where thousands of weary and hungry people needed to be fed. Yet there was almost no food on hand. The way Jesus responds to the situation, versus the way the disciples do, shows us how giving thanks is way more than just being polite. It's a key that opens the doors of Heaven to shift things from lack into a bounty of abundance and plenty.

BREAK FREE OF THE FEAR AND FRUSTRATION OF PERCEIVED LACK

When the Lord saw that there were hungry people, His response was compassion. He wanted to care for them and provide for them (see Matthew 15:32). His thoughts were all about them. He saw there was a need, and His response was *let's meet the need*.

The disciples' response is very different. They immediately go into a panic saying, *"Where would we get enough food out here in the wilderness for such a huge crowd?"* (Matthew 15:33 NLT). They weren't focused on the need. They weren't focused on the people. They weren't even focused on the Lord. They were focused on their total inability to come up with what would be required to feed thousands of people. They didn't have it. And they had no idea where they could possibly get it.

Jesus saw what was happening. He saw that the disciples were gripped by the fear and frustration of perceived lack. They were believing a lie that they didn't have enough of what was needed for the situation. So the Lord tried to shift their focus from what they didn't have to what they did have. He asked, *"How many loaves [of bread] do you have?"* (Matthew 15:34 AMP). They reported that they only had seven loaves, and *"a few small fish."* They were murmuring and complaining about how little they had, because their focus was still on their insufficiency in the natural, as opposed to the abundance that was available to them in their relationship with their heavenly Father through the gift of His Son.

The disciples didn't know it, but they were falling into one of the enemy's favorite traps for us. He loves to get us so focused on what we don't currently have, that we lose sight of the abundance the Lord has blessed us with. The enemy has been using this trick since the beginning.

In the Garden, Adam and Eve had the fullness of relationship, friendship, and fellowship with God. And in that fullness of relationship, they also had the fullness of provision. There was nothing that they lacked. They enjoyed a cornucopia of plenty in all things. All of creation was at their disposal. And when it came to food, they had the banquet of banquets and buffet of buffets (see Genesis 1:29). They could eat of anything and everything. Except for one fruit on one tree that the Lord had warned them about (see Genesis 3:2-3). Think about that for a second. Everything in all creation was theirs. Except one thing. One. And that one thing is what the enemy suckered Eve into focusing on.

Instead of giving thanks to God for all of the abundance at her disposal, Eve chose to focus on the one thing that was not hers. In focusing on what she did not have, as opposed to seeing all that God had blessed her with, her heart and mind hardened toward the Lord, and the place of plenty—the Garden of Eden—ended up being closed off to her.

The enemy still loves to tempt God's children to focus on what it looks like we don't have in the moment so that we miss all that is available to us in the Lord. He loves to sucker us into murmuring and complaining about perceived lack because he knows that it shuts the door on the abundance of Heaven that is always ours through Christ.

When the bills are piling up, the enemy wants us to focus on the current lack of our bank account. He will do whatever he can to get our eyes off the truth that God will meet all our needs according to His riches in glory (see Philippians 4:19).

When there is a daunting problem in front of us, the enemy wants us to focus on how there seems to be no solution. He wants us anxious and tense, as opposed to calmly expectant that God promises to provide the wisdom we need to see something good come out of any challenge we are facing (see James 1:5 and Romans 8:28).

When we are having an argument with our spouse, the enemy wants us totally focused on that one area of disagreement so that we forget all the reasons God brought the two of us together in the first place.

And all too often we jump right in and go along with the enemy's plan. Just like Eve did in the Garden. And the disciples did in Matthew 15. We allow ourselves to get so focused on what we don't seem to have in the moment that we totally lose track of all that is ours in Christ. We eat of the tree of anxiety and fear and frustration and despair. As opposed to banqueting on the buffet of His trustworthiness, faithfulness and abundance of every good thing that He has blessed us with. The power of giving thanks helps shift that.

GIVING THANKS BRINGS INCREASE

Let's take a closer look at how Jesus responded to feeding thousands of people when it looks like there were *only* seven loaves and a *few small* fish on hand.

*Jesus told all the people to sit down on the ground. Then he took the seven loaves and the fish, **thanked God for them**, and broke them into pieces. He gave them to the disciples, who distributed the food to the crowd* (Matthew 15:35-36 NLT).

Jesus's response to the seven loaves and the few fish was the exact opposite of the disciples' panic and anxiety. He didn't murmur. He didn't complain. He was hopeful. He was expectant. He was confident that all was well. So much so that He told the people to sit down on the ground and get ready for a picnic.

Jesus chose not to see what was on hand as lack. He chose to see it as a sign that His heavenly Father was already providing. Sure in the natural this was nowhere near enough to feed everyone there. Not even close. But Jesus wasn't looking to the natural. He was looking to His Father, and the abundant Kingdom of Heaven that Jesus knew He was plugged into here on earth. That's why He took what they had on hand and THANKED GOD for it. He wasn't saying, "Well this is better than nothing, and at least a few people will eat." No. Jesus knew the power of giving thanks. He knew that when we give thanks for what we have, it opens a divine realm of increase and multiplication. Which is exactly what happened.

They all ate as much as they wanted. Afterward, the disciples picked up seven large baskets of leftover food. There were 4,000 men who were fed that day, in addition to all the women and children (Matthew 15:37-38 NLT).

The power of giving thanks multiplied seven loaves and a few small fish into a massive catered banquet for thousands. Everyone there ate their fill, and there was still food left over. Why? Because of the power of giving thanks.

Think of it in the natural. Imagine that you had a friend who needed to come up with $25,000 for a down payment on a house. If you gave that friend $100 to get started, and the friend looked at it and said, "That's it? Just $100? That's nowhere near enough! I need lots more than that! This is no help at all!" That kind of response would probably not open up your floodgates to want to bless them with more. Right?

But now imagine if the friend responded with heartfelt gratitude, and said something like, "You are such a good friend. You are always there for me. Thank you so much for this gift!" You would probably be touched by their appreciation, and might even sow more if you had it to give.

Giving thanks, even in the natural, can be a powerful thing. Even more so in the spirit because in the spirit when we give thanks to God, we're not charming Him or trying to get Him to give us more of what we need. We are thanking Him for what we know He has already given us, even though we have not yet seen it fully in the natural. We give thanks for what we have, because we know what we have in Christ is even more than what we have on hand.

The increase and multiplication doesn't come because we've been polite little boys or girls so our Daddy now gives us another serving of something we need. Increase and multiplication break forth because we are tapping into what we know is ours in Christ beyond what we currently have on hand in the natural.

The enemy wants us to see *not-enough* and panic. Jesus wants us to see, by His example in Matthew 15, that no matter what we have on hand, we can be grateful for the *more-than-enough* we have through relationship with our Father. When we give thanks in the face of temporary not-enough, we are acknowledging and unlocking the realm of divine plenty.

GIVING THANKS INITIATES INCREASE

I had a very personal experience with the power of giving thanks and how it can shift us from an anxious, fearful mindset of lack, and unlock a supernatural realm of increase. It was years ago when I was at an extreme low point in a twelve-year battle to overcome many mysterious and debilitating health challenges. Most days I was so sick and so weak I could barely lift my head.

One morning I was telling the Lord how scared and discouraged I was, because it seemed like nothing was working or helping. No doctor had helped. No medicine had helped. None of the many, many treatments or procedures had helped. At that point, it didn't even feel like prayer was helping.

The Lord lovingly but firmly interrupted my murmurings of self-pity and invited me to thank Him for the strength I had in my body at that moment. I was actually offended by the suggestion. My thought was, *What strength? I can barely lift my head!*

Again, He lovingly but firmly invited me to thank Him for the strength I did have.

Almost begrudgingly I started to do so. I thanked Him for the strength I'd had to get out of bed that morning. Then I thanked Him for the strength I'd had to walk from the bedroom to the kitchen and put the kettle on. Then I thanked Him that I'd had enough strength to take my cup of tea and go sit in my prayer chair.

Much to my surprise as I was thanking Him for the strength I did have, I could feel a shift beginning to take place. The biggest shift was out of self-pity and fear into a genuine gratitude of knowing that the Lord was with me in all I was dealing with. I became deeply grateful for what strength was in my body. I even thanked Him that I had the strength to breathe in and out, form words, and give Him thanks. That initiated something. It wasn't as immediate as the loaves and fish. But multiplication and increase came.

Over the next days, weeks, and months, the more I thanked the Lord for the strength and health and vigor and vitality I had, the more and more of it I actually began to experience in my body. Giving thanks brought forth a shift that no doctor, medicine, or treatment facility had yet been able to. And now here I sit, years later, healthy and strong.

> Giving thanks opens the floodgates of God's goodness.

Let's end this chapter where we began. With Psalm 107:1. We give thanks to the Lord, because He is good. That's really what the power of giving thanks is all about. That's why giving thanks brings forth increase and multiplication. When we give thanks, we are bringing our faith in God's goodness into the situation. We are acknowledging, inviting, and welcoming His copious, abundant, generous, everlasting, overflowing, never-lacking, fullness of goodness.

There may be times our circumstances don't look good. There may be times our bank balance doesn't look good. And there may be times that a medical report or something else in our lives doesn't look good. We must never allow ourselves to get so focused on those things that don't look good, that we forget God is good. That He is for us. That He is with us. And in the certainty and goodness of our relationship with Him, we can also be certain of the plenty of His provision.

Thank You, Lord!

ACTIVATE THE POWER OF GIVING THANKS

The next time you find yourself in a situation where it seems like you don't have enough of something to meet the need, remember the power of giving thanks.

Focus on what you *do* have and set your eyes on Heaven, remembering that in Christ you actually have everything. As you give thanks for that, expect your increase. It may come immediately. It may come over time. But it will come. Not because you're *earning* more from God by giving thanks, but because you are activating all that He is, all that He's done, and everything that He has given you when you thank Him for what you have.

The following are some more keys to help you unlock the power of giving thanks.

1. Remember: In Christ, you never really lack anything.

Whenever it looks like you don't have enough of something in the natural—whether it's food, finances, favor, wisdom, strength, or anything else—choose to respond like Jesus, not the disciples. Refuse a lack mentality. Bind fear and anxiety if you need to. And remember that you have been given everything pertaining to life and godliness in Christ. In other words, focus on the truth that whatever you have need of in the natural, you already have in Christ.

2. Remember: No need is too great or too difficult.

If the situation seems impossible, think about the finished work of the Cross. When it came to saving ourselves, we were completely and totally insufficient. We were lacking in every way. But Heaven was not. The abundance of God's goodness stepped out of Heaven into this realm and provided for us what we could not do for ourselves. The truth of Romans 8:32 declares the gift of God's Son is proof that there is nothing God would ever withhold from us. Now you can be certain that whatever you need, in whatever situation you are facing, God has it and will give it to you. That should get the "Thank You" stream flowing!

3. Repent of any murmuring and complaining.

Murmuring and complaining are signs of fear, anxiety, self-pity, and choosing to believe that lack is our portion. They work the exact opposite of giving thanks. But fear not, the blood of Jesus is sufficient for this too. Simply repent for any murmuring or complaining. Plead the blood of Jesus over it all. And thank the Lord for His forgiveness.

4. Lift up your eyes and see.

Ask God for the grace to see beyond the need and the seeming lack in the natural. Remember that your Source is not the natural realm, but the abundance of Heaven where there is no lack of any kind. Heaven is a realm of more-than-enough, and you are plugged into it through Christ (see Ephesians 1:3; 2 Peter 1:3; Matthew 6:33). Jesus did not look to the natural when He needed to feed thousands in Matthew 15. He looked to Heaven. And so should we.

5. Give thanks to God for what you have.

Remember that what you have on hand is not all that you have in Christ. Choose to see what you do have on hand as a sign that God has already started providing. Thank Him for it. And even if you think you have absolutely nothing of what you need on hand, thank Him for the faith for being able to see beyond the natural to what is yours in the spirit. Then begin to thank the Lord for all that you know is yours in Christ.

– 12 –

Power of Forgiveness

If you forgive the sins of any,
their sins have been forgiven
them; if you retain the sins of
any, they have been retained
(John 20:23 NASB).

IF you have any question whatsoever about the power of forgiveness, think about this: You're not going to hell. Forgiveness is so powerful that it completely, utterly, and totally changed your life for all eternity.

Most Christians understand how powerful Jesus's forgiveness is. But He wants us to understand that forgiveness is not only a realm of power that He can move in. He wants us to realize that the power of forgiveness is a realm that's available to us all.

Look at John 20:23, the Scripture that opened this chapter. In that part of John 20, Jesus the victorious risen Lord is launching the disciples out to change the world. As He does this, the very first thing He talks to them about is how important and powerful forgiveness is. Yes, of course, He is releasing them to preach the Gospel and declare to all people in all places that through Him their sins are forgiven and they may have eternal life. But He's also letting the disciples know how important it is that *they* move in the power of forgiveness. He is letting them know that there's also power when *they* forgive those who have sinned against them. And that there are dire consequences when they don't forgive.

This had nothing to do with Jesus making the disciples mini-messiahs. There is only One Messiah. There is only One Lamb of God who takes away all the sins of all the world. There is only One name that can be called upon to be saved and have our sins removed as far as the east is from the west. That Messiah, that One, that name is Jesus Christ, and Him alone.

When Jesus spoke to the disciples about the importance and impact of them forgiving sins, He was not making the disciples junior-saviors. He was opening their eyes, and ours as well, to the reality that because of all He has done, all His disciples are empowered to walk in His authority and do the works that He did. Including moving in the power of forgiveness.

FORGIVE OTHERS AS YOU HAVE BEEN FORGIVEN

John 20:23 wasn't the first time Jesus highlighted the importance and power of forgiveness to the disciples. He also pointed it out in Matthew 6:5-14, when He was teaching them how to position themselves in prayer to see Heaven invade earth through their lives. The Lord's Prayer begins with a section acknowledging who God is and what He wants to do (see Matthew 6:9-10). Then there is an expectant petition for His provision (see Matthew 6:11). But the very first thing mentioned for the disciples to do is all about choosing to operate in the power of forgiveness (see Matthew 6:12).

Jesus wanted the disciples to know that His forgiveness—and all the blessings and benefits it makes available to us—is a free gift that can simply be received. But He also wanted them to catch that one of the keys to becoming an expression of Him is agreeing to be like Him, and not hold anyone's sins against them.

If we, as disciples of Jesus Christ, want to partner with the Lord to see Heaven invade earth through our lives, we need to move in the power of forgiveness.

REFUSING TO FORGIVE CAN DETER A MOVE OF GOD

Let's look at the power of forgiveness from another angle. In Luke 9:51-56, Scripture reveals how unforgiveness can actually get in the way of what the Lord would like to do in the lives of those around us.

Jesus and the disciples were headed to Jerusalem. They planned on stopping at a Samaritan village along the way (see Luke 9:51-52). When Jesus sent some of the disciples ahead to help prepare for His arrival, the Samaritans refused to have anything to do with them. They were offended because Jesus planned to continue on to Jerusalem (see Luke 9:53). There was a whole history of offense and bitterness between the Jews of Jerusalem and the Samaritans. Instead of forgiving the Jews and letting go of the offense, the Samaritans chose to hold on to it all. Refusing to forgive cost the Samaritans a visitation of the Lord. Who knows what miracles, signs, wonders, and more would have broken out in their village if they simply had chosen to forgive?

But it doesn't end there.

James and John heard about all this, and instead of forgiving the Samaritans for their offense, the two disciples got offended by what happened. They actually asked Jesus if He wanted them to call down fire on the Samaritan village to burn them all up (see Luke 9:54). Jesus's response was to rebuke them (see Luke 9:55). A few translations end there, but several others including AMP, ESV, KJV, NKJV, and NLT go into a bit more detail sharing not only what Jesus did, but also what He said. His response to James and John:

> *You don't realize what your hearts are like. For the Son of Man has not come to destroy people's lives, but to save them* (Luke 9:55-56 NLT).

Jesus immediately pointed to the condition of their hearts. He was opening their eyes to the trap of unforgiveness. He wanted them to see that unforgiveness closes off the heart and keeps us from being a gate of Heaven to earth. He wanted them to wake up to the truth that you can't fight offense with more offense. You can't overcome darkness with more darkness. The way to bring healing, life, transformation—the Kingdom!—into a situation mired in the hurt, pain, and bitterness of unforgiveness, is to choose to move in the opposite spirit. You choose not to destroy, but to save. You choose not to hold sins against someone, but forgive.

Forgiveness, is an essential aspect of partnering with God to see His Kingdom come and His will be done on earth as it is in Heaven (see Matthew 6:10-12).

Forgiveness has the power to heal and transform.

My father and I have always been very different people. He is an M.I.T. and Johns Hopkins-educated engineer. I was a sensitive, creative kid who preferred the world of my imagination to any nuts-and-bolts reality. We never really understood each other or saw eye-to-eye on anything. And for most of our lives we didn't get along. It wasn't so much that we had knockdown drag-out yelling and screaming matches. We just sort of gave up on trying to connect with each other in any meaningful way pretty early on.

In my mid-twenties, I started to realize how much hurt, anger, and animosity I had toward my father. But I also had no real interest in trying to do anything about it. I thought that nothing would ever change, so what was the point? I told myself that I was fine continuing what I felt was a very justified simmering distance toward my father. I went on like that for most of my adult life. Then in my late thirties I got saved through a sovereign encounter with the Lord who had a very different take on it all.

I had only been a Christian for about a month when the Lord took me into a deep encounter that firmly rooted me in a profound revelation of Him as my heavenly Father. From that moment on I have always been certain of my sonship, and secure in the love and acceptance of God as my Father. But there came a time when He also wanted me to address my relationship with my earthly father. I'm not proud of this, but my initial response was to think, *Why bother?*

My father and I had reached a sort of détente over the years. We could talk occasionally. We could even see each other on a holiday every once in a while. As long as we limited our time together and avoided any topics of substance, we were fine. Usually.

I believe that for a while we both tried in our own ways. But we were so different, I don't think we could ever really see the other person trying. And then we got to a point where it was just easier to not expect anything from each other. After years like that, I told myself I was good with it all, that it was easier that way. But the Lord knew better. And He had something better for both me and my father.

I remember the day the Lord asked me a question about what I thought the root issue was between my father and me. I was sitting in my prayer chair, and pondered that for quite some time. Eventually I answered, "We're just so different. I wasn't very good at, or very interested in, the things that seemed to matter most to him. All my life, way down deep, I guess I felt like I wasn't the son that he really wanted." I could feel the truth of it. And the hurt. The Lord comforted me, reminding me of my great worth and value in His eyes, and the certainty of my place in His heart. In that moment, I forgave my father.

Then the Lord whispered another question, *"Do you ever think your dad was hurt by all the ways you communicated to him that he was not the father you wanted?"*

All of a sudden I could see it so clearly. For decades, I'd only been able to view things, and feel things, and think about things from my perspective. But there in the comfort of the Lord's embrace, I was able to get past the ways I'd been hurt, and could see so vividly all the ways I had hurt my father. How I'd subtly, and not so subtly, over and over again throughout the years, communicated my dissatisfaction with him. My heart broke. I knew I needed to make things right.

A few days later I connected with my dad. He was still not sure what to make of my commitment to Christ back then, so I skipped everything about the encounter. I also never brought up any of the ways I had been hurt—after all, I had forgiven him. I simply apologized to him for the things I had done over the years. And I asked him to forgive me. When he did, things began to change between us. Not totally right away. But significantly over time.

My dad and I are still quite different. But these days, we genuinely enjoy one another. We look forward to talking. We look forward to catching up. We look forward to the times we get to spend together. I love my dad. I appreciate the man he is. I appreciate the father he is. I appreciate who he is and what he's like. I know I'm better off for having him in my life, and for having him as my father.

There was a time I couldn't imagine thinking any of that, let alone saying it. For decades my heart was closed off to him. Perhaps justifiably so. But the Kingdom doesn't come, and God's will isn't done through hearts that are "justifiably" hard. His Kingdom comes and His will is done through those who are willing to forgive. Heaven is released through us when we don't look for reasons to destroy, but opportunities to heal. His light breaks forth in the midst of darkness when we choose not to call down fire, but to move in love. That's the power of forgiveness. It can heal decades of wounds and totally transform even the most broken of relationships.

DON'T BELIEVE THE LIE

The enemy knows how powerful forgiveness is. He is very aware how completely, utterly, and totally it dismantles his works on earth. That's why he tries so hard to keep us trapped in unforgiveness. Call it offense. Call it bitterness. Call it justified. Whatever you call it, it's the refusal to forgive.

The reason why sometimes it seems so hard to forgive is because the enemy lies to us. He hisses into our thoughts that if we forgive the people who have wronged us, we're saying that what they did was okay. That it was "no big deal." How could we possibly forgive the one who failed us, betrayed us, rejected us, abused us, abandoned us, stole from us, lied to us, or worse? We do it by realizing that forgiveness is not about saying that what was done was "okay," it's about removing the impact of those hurts, betrayals, rejections, and wrongs from our lives and our hearts.

ACTIVATE THE POWER OF FORGIVENESS

When Jesus forgave us at the Cross, He was not saying that sin was "no big deal." He was removing sin's ability to continue to separate us from Him and all the good things He has for us. Unforgiveness isolates. It cuts off. It keeps us from being who we truly are in Christ. The power of forgiveness changes all of that. It shifts us from a punishment mindset to a redemptive one. It shifts us from worrying about protecting ourselves, to being willing to contend for others—even ones who have hurt us. The power of forgiveness moves us from the pain of the past into a glorious future of being more and more like Jesus.

So let's get you activated in the power of forgiveness.

1. Be willing to forgive.

It all begins with being willing to forgive. Remember what we talked about, forgiving doesn't mean what was done to you was okay. Forgiving means what was done to you will no longer impact you. Even with that, if you're wrestling to forgive, remember that Jesus has forgiven the person. If He has done it, then you can too. Because you can do all things through Christ (see Philippians 4:13).

2. Ask the Holy Spirit to search your heart.

With some people, it will be obvious that you need to forgive them. You probably already know you heart isn't quite right toward them. They're the people who when somebody mentions them, you can't wait to speak up about the things they've done, or the bad people they are. Others we need to forgive aren't always so obvious. Maybe because what happened is years in the past. Or perhaps you've told yourself, over and over again, that you're okay with it all. Ask the Holy Spirit to search your heart. You don't have to go digging through your past, but if the Holy Spirit highlights someone, choose to forgive.

3. Declare forgiveness out loud.

It's good to think about forgiving someone, but it's even more powerful to declare it out loud. Remember the power of decree. You can say it to the person, but you don't have to—especially if you need to maintain safe boundaries, or the person has passed away. It's okay to declare it between just you and the Lord. But know that something happens when you declare out loud, "I forgive...." It releases the power of forgiveness into the atmosphere.

4. The power of forgiveness is not based on feelings.

Be aware that you may not feel different right away. There will be times when you forgive and feel a weight lifted off your heart or a wall removed between you and the person. But other times you won't feel a thing. That doesn't mean the power of forgiveness isn't working. Like every realm of power available to you in Jesus Christ, you access the power of forgiveness by faith. Forgive by faith not by feelings. When you do, you're activating the power. The feelings will come in time.

5. Forgiveness may not always be a one-time thing.

Know that it's okay to declare your forgiveness over and over until you feel a shift. There are people I have forgiven again and again. Not because I was dredging up the past, but because I knew every time I did I was removing more and more of the hurt. The power of forgiveness works as soon as you use it, but there's nothing wrong with using the power again and again until you also sense the freedom it has given you.

– 13 –

Power to
Make Wealth

But you are to remember

the Lord your God, for it is

He who is giving you power

to make wealth, in order

to confirm His covenant...

(Deuteronomy 8:18 NASB).

GOD is very generous. He gave us the gift of His Son. He has given us eternal life. He has given us the certainty of His presence. He has given us every spiritual blessing in heavenly places here on earth. As well as everything pertaining to life and godliness. Plus there are all the fruit and gifts of the Spirit He has bestowed upon us.

On top of all that He has already given us, we are also promised in Philippians 4:19 that God will meet all our needs according to His riches in glory in Christ Jesus.

But wait...there's even more!

Our giving God even goes beyond all of that. He is so generous that He has provided a realm of blessing for you that even exceeds Him faithfully meeting your needs. It is a realm where He empowers you to walk in abundance so plentiful that you're able to become a blessing to others. In this realm, you—just like your heavenly Father in whose image you are made—are so well supplied that you're able to generously help meet the needs of other people, families, churches, missions, even cities or nations.

He has given you all of this by giving you the power to make wealth.

POVERTY IS NOT HOLY

Before we start to unlock this realm of power for you, we need to address a lie that infiltrated the church somewhere along the way. In some circles of Christianity, there is a belief that being poor is some kind of virtue. That's simply not true. Poverty is not holy. Lack is not a good thing. I have served in many areas, regions, and even nations of the world that have been ravaged by poverty. It is debilitating, devastating, and even deadly.

Maybe this lie crept in because when Jesus sent His disciples out into the world to preach the Gospel, He told them not to take any money with them (see Luke 10:4). But I would like to point out that Jesus was not conscripting believers into a life of lack, He was assuring them that they could rely on their heavenly Father to meet all their needs every step of the way.

After all, Jesus had personally instructed many of these same disciples to believe for *"on earth as it is in heaven"* (see Matthew 6:10). There is no lack in Heaven. Heaven is supernaturally abundant. Even its streets are pure gold (see Revelation 21:21). Resources and provision are not an issue in Heaven. At all. So why would the same Lord who instructed His disciples to pray for it to be on earth as it is in heaven, consign them to be in lack? He wouldn't. And He didn't. Jesus was not initiating a Gospel of holy destitution. He was launching His disciples out into a life of supernatural provision. He was letting them know that they would never need to look to the world's system, values, compromises, or schemes for their needs to be met. Their generous and abundant heavenly Father would more than look after them wherever they went.

More likely this lie about poverty being holy has to do with confusion surrounding First Timothy 6:10 (NASB) when Paul told his young associate that:

> *The love of money is a root of all sorts of evil, and some by longing for it have wandered away from the faith and pierced themselves with many griefs.*

Please take note that Paul did not say that money was the root of all sorts of evil. It was the *love* of money that was the problem. Money is simply a tool. A resource. We can use it. We can even appreciate it. But we are for sure not to love it. And we should never ascribe worth or value according to how much money we or others have. We love God, not money. We serve God, and use the resources He blesses us with to serve His purposes and the needs of those around us.

I've seen what the love of money can do. In all the years I worked in Southeast Asia to help bring an end to human trafficking, I saw many heartbreaking and horrific things. Ultimately what was behind every single one of them was the love of money. Loving money more than righteousness. Loving money more than all those trafficked and abused women and children. Loving money more than life itself. That love of money was the root of all sorts of evil that we encountered and worked to overcome each and every day we were there.

But money itself? Again, it is simply a tool.

> ## We are to care for the poor, not be poor.

We were able to help many of those women and children because of the money the Lord had blessed us with. We built homes and schools and medical facilities for the little ones who were delivered from that terrible life. We were able to start micro-enterprise training programs for the women, as well as business start-up ventures so they could step into alternative means of making a living and caring for their families. We were able to establish and help ministries, churches, Bible studies, and community outreach programs to revive and restore every rescued life, as well as help interrupt the cycle of poverty that often led to so many being trafficked in the first place. That was all done with money. Money that served life and love and good, as opposed to a love of money that is a root of evil.

Another reason we can be certain that poverty is not holy is because the Lord tells us in multiple places throughout both the Old and New Testaments that we should care for the poor. He doesn't say we are to *be* poor. He says we are to *help* the poor. If poverty was such a glorious thing, why would He remind us so frequently to help those in need?

We need to be willing to be blessed, so that we can be a blessing (see Genesis 12:2). We need to know how to freely receive so that we can freely give (see Matthew 10:8).

I hope you are seeing that God is not about poverty or lack. He is about abundance and plenty (see John 10:10). He is about multiplication and increase of every good thing. So let's get back to the power God has given you to make wealth.

PROVISION IS GOOD, PROVIDING IS EVEN BETTER

The Scripture we started with, Deuteronomy 8:18, says that God has given you the power to make wealth. What I want you to see is that the Lord says something more than simply promising to give you wealth. He clearly promises that He has given you the power to *make* wealth. It's not that God can't drop a bunch of money into your savings or checking account. He can. I've seen it happen. Multiple times. But that's God giving you finances. Which is great, and part of His promise to always meet your needs according to His riches in glory that we looked at in Philippians 4:19.

But in Deuteronomy 8:18, God is pointing out to you that He has done something beyond making Himself a divine ATM you can cry out to when you need a provisional miracle. God wants to open your eyes to the supernatural reality that there's a realm of power you can access so that you will never be in need of a provisional miracle again. This supernatural power shifts you from needing divine provision to partnering with God to become one of His divine providers on earth. This is the power to *make* wealth.

The Lord did this with the disciples in the Gospels when He asked them to feed the multitudes. At first they had no idea what to do. All they could see was the massive provisional needs of the 5,000 and 4,000 people. What's interesting is that Jesus did not simply have food rain from the sky, or have a bunch of huge carts from a nearby market all of a sudden show up and dump out tons of food. Instead, He mentored the disciples on how to enter into a realm where they could work with what they had and make wealth. The wealth of food that met every need of everyone there, along with baskets of leftovers, all came forth at the hands of the disciples.

They did it. And so can you.

ACTIVATE THE POWER TO MAKE WEALTH

Most of the keys we are about to discuss are things you're well aware of. A few of them you may have even dismissed as Old Testament, legalistic, or not necessary. But you will see as we look at each key that those things are not true. Those are lies the devil has been using in an attempt to limit the provision and wealth that you walk in. Each of these keys are scriptural truths that are biblically proven to help you step into the power to make wealth.

1. Tithing.

The tithe is not an Old Testament religious requirement. Choosing to tithe does not put you under the law. The tithe was actually initiated by Abram before the Mosaic Law was ever proclaimed (see Genesis 14:20). The tithe is a way of honoring the Lord. It declares that you know who your Source is, and that you trust in His steady flow of provision in all things. And according to Malachi 3:10, when you tithe it actually works to open the windows of Heaven over your life and establish a flow of blessing so abundant you will not be able to contain it. In other words, when you faithfully tithe to honor the Lord, you will be so blessed that you will be able to become a blessing. That's making wealth.

Over the years I have heard many people say things like, "I will tithe when I can afford to." That type of thinking is actually a trap of the enemy that keeps you in lack. The attitude there is that you are waiting for God to do something before you choose to honor Him, as opposed to tapping into a realm of increase and abundance by showing honor and appreciation for what He has done. When a believer refuses to tithe, they are refusing one of the main tools the Lord has blessed us with to make wealth.

2. Sowing and reaping.

Years ago a minister with whom I often did events asked me why I loved receiving offerings so much. I told him it was because I knew when I gave people an opportunity to sow into really good Kingdom ground, I was actually giving them the opportunity to make wealth. It's the same reason I love giving into offerings. When we sow generously, we reap abundantly (see Luke 6:38).

Just like in the natural, sowing leads to reaping. Plant an apple seed, and you get way more than one apple. You get a tree filled with apples. And every one of those apples is filled with apple seeds. One seed sown, reaped a wealth of apples and seeds! It works the same way as a Kingdom principle. Need a wealth of favor in your life? Start sowing favor to those around you. Need a wealth of finances? Start sowing funds into good Kingdom works. And remember to be intentional in both the sowing and the reaping. When you sow, do it cheerfully, generously, and mindfully (see 2 Corinthians 9:6-11). Know what you are sowing, and why you are sowing it. Then be intentional about reaping the increase. Be in faith about it. Declare it. Steward it in prayer. And receive by faith. No farmer plants a seed without expecting a harvest. So when you sow, expect to reap.

3. Gratitude and thanksgiving.

Remember a few paragraphs back where we talked about Jesus mentoring the disciples in how to tap into the power to make wealth so that they could feed the multitudes? Take some time to read those passages of Scripture in Matthew 14:13-21, 15:32-39 and Mark 6:30-44, 8:1-13, as well as in John 6:1-15. What you will notice is that the first thing the disciples did was murmur and complain. They focused on what they didn't have, told Jesus there was nowhere to get that amount of food; and even if there was, they didn't have enough money to buy it. They also told the Lord that the whole thing was, "Impossible!" Jesus shifts them out of this negativity and lack-focus by asking them what they do have. When they bring it to Him, He is not moved by how little or small or few any of it is. He simply gives thanks to His Father for what they had (see John 6:11). A wealth of food comes forth. Being grateful and giving thanks for what you have taps you into the power to make wealth.

4. Don't miss opportunities to be generous.

Being generous is a huge key to tapping into the power to make wealth. Look at what it says in Second Corinthians 9:10-11 (TPT): *"...the harvest of your generosity will grow. You will be abundantly enriched in every way as you give generously on every occasion...."* Notice that it specifically points out that the harvest of your generosity will grow, and that the key to unlocking abundant enrichment is to give generously on every occasion. Be on the lookout for opportunities that the Lord blesses you with to be generous. Whether it's offerings, tithes, sharing your lunch with someone, giving a kind word where needed, buying a coffee for the person behind you in line, giving of your time to someone when you're busy, sharing wisdom, showing appreciation. Whatever it is, don't miss those chances to be generous. Each of them is the Lord helping you tap into the power to make wealth. Choosing to be generous whenever you are given the opportunity brings forth abundant enrichment. Which means you will have even more to be generous with when you have the next opportunity to be generous—bringing forth an even greater harvest from your generosity. These harvests grow and grow. That's the power to make wealth!

– 14 –

Truly, Truly

Truly, truly I say to you,

the one who believes in Me,

the works that I do, he will do

also; and greater works than

these he will do; because

I am going to the Father

(John 14:12 NASB).

DO you believe in Jesus? Well then, according to what He declared in John 14:12, because you are *"one who believes,"* you will do the works that He did while He was here on behalf of the Father.

As amazing as that is, what's even more profound is that in that same passage, Jesus goes on to declare that believers are called to even *"greater works."* He's letting His followers know that a day is coming when His work here will be finished, and He will go to be with the Father. That's when the church will become the Body of Christ on earth, continuing to put the reality of the Father and His Kingdom on display in notable and remarkable ways.

Those are the days we are in. That's what you are called to do. That's who you truly are in Christ. Or as Jesus Himself put it, "Truly, truly."

More than anything else, what I want you to take from the time we have spent together in this book is the Kingdom truth that *you are powerful.* You are here to represent and re-present the Father to everyone you meet, everywhere you go, and in every set of circumstances you find yourself.

You are God's dominion steward on earth.

You have a key role to play for Him in these historic and epic days.

And you've been equipped and empowered with everything you need to be one of His mighty difference-makers and solution-bringers.

The entire universe is waiting in anticipation for you to realize who you truly are, and all that you carry. The earth is waiting (see Romans 8:19). Heaven is waiting (see Romans 8:26). And something deep inside of you is waiting too (see Romans 8:23). Today is your day to step into the realms of power you have in Christ and become the power-packed witness of Him you are meant to be.

The past is past. If you've been hidden or overlooked in the past, those days are done. If you were hesitant or unsure in the past, those days are done. If, in the past, you thought the miraculous, supernatural, power-packed aspects of the Kingdom were for others, you now know the truth. This is your time. This is your moment. This is your chance to step out into what you were created for, and begin to walk in all you are empowered to be.

Truly, truly.

ACTIVATE YOUR GOD-GIVEN POWER

So let's look at a few final keys to help you get activated in the realms of power you have been blessed with in Christ.

1. You have the power.

This whole book has been pointing out realms of power available to you in Christ. Your Bible does the same thing. The Lord even devoted an entire book in the New Testament—*the Acts of the Apostles*—to make it clear what you carry as a believer. So the question is no longer whether or not you have the power, it's whether or not you will use it. Let's settle that, as well. Decree this over yourself, *"I believe I am powerful in Christ, and I will move in that power to glorify Him each and every day!"*

2. Practice is good.

In First Corinthians 12:31 and 14:1, the apostle Paul instructs believers to earnestly desire and zealously cultivate the gifts of the Spirit. He is telling the church that we are meant to be active in the realms of power that we have been blessed with. We are to cultivate them. Grow in them.

Or, to put it another way, we are to practice. How does a worship leader get better at leading worship? By singing or playing the piano or guitar every single day. How does an evangelist get better at leading people to the Lord? By going out on the streets and talking with the lost again and again. How does an intercessor get better at interceding and leading prayer meetings? By praying.

Similarly, there is no better way to get more seasoned in realms of power than by moving in those realms. You may be brilliant and anointed the very first time you step out. And you may not. Regardless, the way you "carve out" a deep, seasoned, realm of power is simply by doing it—again and again. When it seems to work, and when it seems not to. Keep at it. Be faithful. Practice!

3. Pick a realm and go for it.

In this book, we looked at 12 different realms of power that are available to you in Christ. If it seems like too much to start developing all of those realms at the same time, then simply focus on one. Reread that chapter again and again. Dig into the Scriptures that were cited. Ask the Holy Spirit to lead you through your own study on that realm of power. Make that your focus. And then, when you're confidently moving in that realm, pick another one to develop. Before you know it, you'll be seasoned in them all.

4. Establish a solid faith circle.

There's a reason the Lord didn't send the original disciples out solo. When we're learning to move in realms of power, it's great to have a faith ally with us along the way. Someone who is there to celebrate when we see God move through us, and who is also there to keep us encouraged if things don't always go the way we're expecting. Of course, we each have the ultimate Faith Ally in the Holy Spirit. He is always ready to help, counsel, encourage, and disciple. In addition to Him, I have found it helpful to have a small, solid circle of faith-filled believers in my life. People like my wife, my spiritual mother, my pastor, and a few brothers who are always willing to remind me who I truly am in Christ, while encouraging me to keep believing, and keep going after all I know I am called to.

5. Be inspired, but don't waste time comparing.

One of the traps we can fall into when we start moving in realms of power is to compare ourselves with others. The Lord will often highlight men or women of God who are moving powerfully in a certain realm (or who did so in church history). Know that they're meant to be inspiring examples of what is available to you in God. They are not meant to be a yardstick to measure yourself by. Usually only one of two things happens when we compare ourselves to others. We either feel we're way ahead of the pack, and flirt with the danger of pride. Or we feel everyone else is more anointed, and we're tempted to give up. Neither is what the Lord has for you.

Be inspired by the great women and men of God throughout church history and on earth today. But don't compare yourself to them. You are on your own personal walk with Jesus. Enjoy it. Know that He is leading you into the great and mighty things you are called to do. It will look different from what others are called to. Which is exactly how it's supposed to be.

Notes

About the Author

ROBERT Hotchkin is the founder of Men on the Frontlines and Robert Hotchkin Ministries. He also serves as a core leader of Patricia King Ministries. Robert hosts the *Heroes Arise* broadcast and has been a regular guest and co-host on GodTV's *Supernatural Life*. His ministry and media inspire believers to grab hold of the finished work of the Cross and walk in the fullness of their authority as Kingdom agents of impact.

You can connect with Robert, as well as continue to receive from him, by visiting his website: RobertHotchkin.com.